Guidance notes for the

Supply Contract

This contract should be used for local and international procurement of high value goods and related services including design

An NEC document

April 2013

Construction Clients' Board endorsement of NEC3

The Construction Clients' Board recommends that public sector organisations use the NEC3 contracts when procuring construction. Standardising use of this comprehensive suite of contracts should help to deliver efficiencies across the public sector and promote behaviours in line with the principles of *Achieving Excellence in Construction.*

Cabinet Office UK

NEC is a division of Thomas Telford Ltd, which is a wholly owned subsidiary of the Institution of Civil Engineers (ICE), the owner and developer of the NEC.

The NEC is a family of standard contracts, each of which has these characteristics:

- Its use stimulates good management of the relationship between the two parties to the contract and, hence, of the work included in the contract.

- It can be used in a wide variety of commercial situations, for a wide variety of types of work and in any location.

- It is a clear and simple document – using language and a structure which are straightforward and easily understood.

NEC3 Supply Contract is one of the NEC family and is consistent with all other NEC3 documents. This document comprises the Supply Contract Guidance Notes. Also available are the Supply Contract Flow Charts.

ISBN (complete box set) 978 0 7277 5867 5
ISBN (this document) 978 0 7277 5931 3
ISBN (Supply Contract) 978 0 7277 5895 8
ISBN (Supply Contract Flow Charts) 978 0 7277 5933 7

First edition 2009
Reprinted 2010
Reprinted with amendments 2013

British Library Cataloguing in Publication Data for this publication is available from the British Library.

Typeset by Academic + Technical, Bristol

Printed and bound in Great Britain by Bell & Bain Limited, Glasgow, UK

CONTENTS

FOREWORD

I was delighted to be asked to write the Foreword for the NEC3 Contracts.

I have followed the outstanding rise and success of NEC contracts for a number of years now, in particular during my tenure as the 146th President of the Institution of Civil Engineers, 2010/11.

In my position as UK Government's Chief Construction Adviser, I am working with Government and industry to ensure Britain's construction sector is equipped with the knowledge, skills and best practice it needs in its transition to a low carbon economy. I am promoting innovation in the sector, including in particular the use of Building Information Modelling (BIM) in public sector construction procurement; and the synergy and fit with the collaborative nature of NEC contracts is obvious. The Government's construction strategy is a very significant investment and NEC contracts will play an important role in setting high standards of contract preparation, management and the desirable behaviour of our industry.

In the UK, we are faced with having to deliver a 15–20 per cent reduction in the cost to the public sector of construction during the lifetime of this Parliament. Shifting mind-set, attitude and behaviour into best practice NEC processes will go a considerable way to achieving this.

Of course, NEC contracts are used successfully around the world in both public and private sector projects; this trend seems set to continue at an increasing pace. NEC contracts are, according to my good friend and NEC's creator Dr Martin Barnes CBE, about better management of projects. This is quite achievable and I encourage you to understand NEC contracts to the best you can and exploit the potential this offers us all.

Peter Hansford

UK Government's Chief Construction Adviser
Cabinet Office

PREFACE

The NEC contracts are the only suite of standard contracts designed to facilitate and encourage good management of the projects on which they are used. The experience of using NEC contracts around the world is that they really make a difference. Previously, standard contracts were written mainly as legal documents best left in the desk drawer until costly and delaying problems had occurred and there were lengthy arguments about who was to blame.

The language of NEC contracts is clear and simple, and the procedures set out are all designed to stimulate good management. Foresighted collaboration between all the contributors to the project is the aim. The contracts set out how the interfaces between all the organisations involved will be managed – from the client through the designers and main contractors to all the many subcontractors and suppliers.

Versions of the NEC contract are specific to the work of professional service providers such as project managers and designers, to main contractors, to subcontractors and to suppliers. The wide range of situations covered by the contracts means that they do not need to be altered to suit any particular situation.

The NEC contracts are the first to deal specifically and effectively with management of the inevitable risks and uncertainties which are encountered to some extent on all projects. Management of the expected is easy, effective management of the unexpected draws fully on the collaborative approach inherent in the NEC contracts.

Most people working on projects using the NEC contracts for the first time are hugely impressed by the difference between the confrontational characteristics of traditional contracts and the teamwork engendered by the NEC. The NEC does not include specific provisions for dispute avoidance. They are not necessary. Collaborative management itself is designed to avoid disputes and it really works.

It is common for the final account for the work on a project to be settled at the time when the work is finished. The traditional long period of expensive professional work after completion to settle final payments just is not needed.

The NEC contracts are truly a massive change for the better for the industries in which they are used.

Dr Martin Barnes CBE

Originator of the NEC contracts

ACKNOWLEDGEMENTS

The first edition of the Supply Contract was produced by the Institution of Civil Engineers through its NEC Panel. It was mainly drafted by P. A. Baird and J. J. Lofty with the assistance of P. Higgins, N. C. Shaw and J. M. Hawkins.

The NEC3 Supply Contract Guidance Notes were produced by the Institution of Civil Engineers and were mainly drafted by P. A. Baird and J. J. Lofty with the assistance of members of the NEC Panel. The Flow Charts were produced by Ross Hayes.

The original NEC was designed and drafted by Dr Martin Barnes then of Coopers and Lybrand with the assistance of Professor J. G. Perry then of the University of Birmingham, T. W. Weddell then of Travers Morgan Management, T. H. Nicholson, Consultant to the Institution of Civil Engineers, A. Norman then of the University of Manchester Institute of Science and Technology and P. A. Baird, then Corporate Contracts Consultant, Eskom, South Africa.

The members of the NEC Panel are:

N. C. Shaw, FCIPS, CEng, MIMechE (Chairman)
F. Alderson, BA (Melb), Solicitor
P. A. Baird, BSc, CEng, FICE, M(SA)ICE, MAPM
M. Codling, BSc, ICIOB, MAPM
L. T. Eames, BSc, FRICS, FCIOB
M. Garratt, BSc(Hons), MRICS, FCIArb
J. J. Lofty, MRICS

NEC Consultant:

R. A. Gerrard, BSc(Hons), FRICS, FCIArb, FCInstCES

Secretariat:

J. M. Hawkins, BA(Hons), MSc
S. Hernandez, BSc, MSc

AMENDMENTS

Full details of all amendments are available on www.neccontract.com.

CHAPTER 1   INTRODUCTION

Background

There are few standard forms for the supply of goods and related services. Most organisations, whether they are sellers or buyers, have their own conditions of sale or purchase that they attempt to incorporate into their contracts for the supply of goods. These conditions are often one sided, favouring the party putting them forward. During the lead up to the formation of a contract, and after, this can lead to what many have called a "battle of the forms" with both parties trying to incorporate their conditions in the contract and the exclusion of the other parties'. In those circumstances it is often difficult to discern exactly what the terms of the supply contract are.

As the benefits of the NEC contracts became increasingly understood and accepted in the changing environment of construction and other industry sectors, the demand arose for a Supply Contract that would be more even handed between the buyer and seller, and therefore bring better certainty as to terms by trying to avoid a battle of the forms. In addition it was felt that a supply contract that was based on the same sound principles as all of the other NEC contracts would help the parties move good practice further down their supply chains.

In response to this demand, the Institution of Civil Engineers have published this NEC3 Supply Contract (SC).

Purpose of these Guidance Notes

The purpose of these guidance notes is to explain the background of the SC, the reasons for some of its provisions and to provide guidance on how to use it. The guidance notes are not contract documents, neither are they part of the SC. They should therefore not be used for legal interpretation of the meaning of the SC.

NEC Objectives

The NEC was drafted with three main objectives

- flexibility,
- clarity,
- stimulus to good management.

These principles have been used in drafting the later contracts. The success of the NEC contracts indicates that these objectives have been achieved.

Flexibility

It was felt that one of the problems with the traditional standard conditions of contract was that there was no simple mechanism to adapt them to the particular circumstances. The result was that they were sometimes used in situations for which they were not suited. Thus the SC is designed for

- use in different commercial situations,
- varying amounts of design by the *Supplier*,
- different methods of pricing and payment,
- appropriate allocation of risk and
- international use.

Clarity

One of the problems with the traditional forms is that the average user finds that they are difficult to understand. Hence NEC drafting was based on the assumption that the contract should be user-friendly and clear. This has been achieved by using short sentences, bullet points and the avoidance of unnecessary legal terms without compromising legal robustness. Subjective terms – so often the cause of disputes – have been avoided as far as possible.

Stimulus to good management

This is one of the most important characteristics of all the NEC contracts. It is founded on the proposition that foresighted co-operative management of the interactions between the parties can shrink the risks inherent in the work. Development in project and supply management techniques has progressed faster than the evolution of forms of contract. Thus the contract includes not only the obligations of the parties but also contractually binding management procedures when various situations arise. Thus in the SC the parties are able to contribute to the management of a supply by improved practices. The parties are motivated by means of the contract to apply such practices to their work.

There are two underlying principles on which the NEC contracts are based and which impact upon the objective of stimulating good management.

- Foresight applied collaboratively mitigates problems and shrinks risk.
- Clear division of function and responsibility helps accountability and motivates people to play their part.

Risk is a major element in contracts and its importance is being increasingly recognised. The NEC contracts allocate clearly these risks between the parties. However, their main task is to reduce the incidence of the risks by application of collaborative foresight. In this way, they aim to improve the outcome of the work generally for parties whose interests might seem to be opposed.

Prominent examples of the management procedures are the early warning procedure, the *Supplier*'s programme and the way in which compensation events are dealt with. Compensation events are events which may lead to a change in payment to the *Supplier* or the timing or both. Generally, assessment of compensation events is based on a forecast of the impact of the event upon the *Supplier*'s costs and timing. Different ways of dealing with the problem may be considered by assessing alternatives. Changes to payment are based upon a quotation. Once the quotation is agreed, the *Supplier* carries the risk of the forecast of cost impact. This arrangement should stimulate foresight, to enable the *Purchaser* to make rational decisions about changes to the work with reasonable certainty of cost and time implications.

The SC makes important use of the programme for the supply and Delivery of the *goods* and *services*. The requirement of an up-to-date and realistic programme maintained by the *Supplier* is used in joint decision-making between the *Supplier* and the *Supply Manager*.

CHAPTER 2   INTRODUCTION TO THE SUPPLY CONTRACT

When should the Supply Contract be used?

The SC is designed to be used for purchase of high value *goods* that are to be used for almost any purpose sourced from anywhere in the world. The *goods* may be wholly or partly designed and manufactured specifically for the contract.

Many applications of the SC will be for orders placed by companies in need of high value plant and machinery for their operations. Such companies could include mining houses or heavy manufacturing and production factories.

However, the *goods* could be required as part of a new project activity where the purchaser is procuring the *goods* for others to install or erect into the project works.

The SC is designed to manage the supply and Delivery of major or complex items of plant and materials or any thing where the value/risk profile is high enough to require active management of the purchase. The SC should not, therefore, be used for straightforward low/medium risk purchases requiring relatively little management such as stock "off-the-shelf" items.

The *Supplier*'s basic obligation is to Provide the Goods and Services; the SC may therefore involve *services* associated with the supply and Delivery but need not do so. Users should note that the SC is not intended to cover installation or erection work done by the *Supplier*.

The SC is not limited to any particular industry; it can be used in many sectors of commercial activity not just engineering, building or construction. The range of complexity of *goods* and the arrangements for the supply is extremely wide. The *goods* are usually manufactured in the *Supplier*'s factories and supplied to the *Purchaser*'s premises or an agreed transport facility. Examples of use of the SC may be for the purchase of:

- Transformers,
- Turbine rotors,
- Rolling Stock,
- Loading Bridges,
- Transmission plant and cable,
- Mining machinery.

The range of *services* associated with the supply and Delivery of the *goods* is also extremely wide. They may include physical work such as final assembly at the delivery place, commissioning and testing or providing knowledge transfer, training and other advice.

Application of the Supply Contract

Although at first reading the SC may appear to be similar to existing bespoke forms of supply-type contracts, to rely on such an impression would be wrong. Most procedures in the SC are based on good management practice and often differ from current practice. This is not a change for the sake of change, since the application of NEC principles in pursuit of its objectives has left very little of conventional practice to be incorporated unchanged.

Users of the SC must, therefore, study it carefully as the words are not simply different expressions of familiar practice. The SC is drafted in a simple and clear style, but its differences from current practice mean that some explanation and consideration of how it will work is necessary when it is first used. That is the purpose of these guidance notes. They are essential reading for those using the SC for the first time. They will continue to be useful in training people coming into the management of supply contracts in how to make best use of the SC.

The SC is also essentially different from the other forms of contract in the NEC family as it has been designed for purchasing *goods* and *services* in a wide variety of sectors. It is essentially a contract for a *Supplier* to supply *goods* to a *Purchaser*, which may include *services* but only where these *services* are directly associated with the supply and Delivery of the *goods*.

It is therefore important to appreciate that the SC

- is not a contract for a project,
- is not intended to involve any installation or erection activity by the *Supplier*,
- can be used at any point in the supply chain with little modification.

The *Purchaser* and *Supplier* may therefore be anyone in the supply chain. In most cases the *Purchaser* is likely to be a client organisation (the *Employer* under the ECC or TSC) or a main contractor organisation (the *Contractor* under the ECC or TSC). The *Supplier* could be a main contractor or subcontractor organisation.

The purchase may be required for a project but does not need to be. In any case the SC is written to be consistent with the other contracts in the NEC family enabling users to benefit from consistent, principles and procedure to meet their requirements.

Some features of the Supply Contract

The SC, like other forms of contract in the NEC family, is designed for use both nationally and internationally. Users contemplating a transaction involving the cross border movement of the *goods* may wish to acquaint themselves with the International Chamber of Commerce (ICC) rules for the interpretation of trade terms (currently Incoterms 2000) which facilitate the conduct of international trade.

The principal obligation of the *Supplier* is to Provide the Goods and Services in accordance with the Goods Information which includes the Supply Requirements for the management of the supply of the *goods*; this is separately defined in the contract.

The Goods Information specifies the *goods* and *services* and the constraints upon how the *Supplier* is to provide them. The Supply Requirements is information which describes the requirements specifically in connection with the management of the supply of the *goods* including transportation and the stated delivery place specified by the *Purchaser*.

A characteristic of supply contracts is the wide variety of delivery places and transport methods that may be appropriate. This is particularly true of international procurements where such terms as EXW (Ex Works), FOB (Free on Board), DDP (Delivered Duty Paid) are frequently used. These terms are not of themselves definitive except by specific reference to published definitions such as those published by the International Chamber of Commerce (ICC). However, direct references to these published definitions in a contract do not fully define all of the necessary obligations for the supply of *goods*.

It is important that the *Purchaser*'s requirements for the supply of the *goods* is definitive on such matters as loading and unloading responsibility, the responsibility for contracting for transportation and the costs of the transport, the location of the delivery place and the arrangements and payments for export and import responsibility. While there is a body of custom and practice that can be appealed to if the parties omit to state the key details, it is obviously best practice to be clear about these matters. This is the purpose of the Supply Requirements in the SC. (See the notes on Supply Requirements in Chapter 4.)

The supply, including transportation, of the *goods* may be all that is required of the *Supplier*, but quite often it is necessary for the *Supplier* to provide *services* such as supervising installation, commissioning or on site testing. To accommodate this, the SC distinguishes between the *goods* and *services* and also between supply (the *goods* are designed, manufactured and transported) and Delivery (when all the work is done including doing any *services* as well as

correcting Defects). The SC allows for multiple Delivery and the respective Delivery Date. (See the explanatory notes on clause 12.5)

The SC includes the Price Schedule which is the payment mechanism for the contract. Unlike other NEC contracts there are no main Options. The Price Schedule is a list of work activities and *goods* and *services* normally prepared by the *Supplier* which he proposes to carry out In Providing the Goods and Services. The Price Schedule is priced by the *Supplier*. It may contain lump sum items or quantified and rated items or any combination of the two.

Key terminology in the Supply Contract

It is important that users appreciate some key words used in the SC that sometimes have multiple meanings or other applications in other contracts and published documents.

The common use of the words, "provide", "supply" and "deliver" can give rise to some overlap and to some users they may even mean the same thing. To maximise clarity and consistency in the SC these words have been used in the following manner.

The word "provide" is used mainly within the defined term 'Provide the Goods and Services' which is the overall contractual obligation principally used in clause 20.1 and in other clauses where the overall responsibility of the *Supplier* needs to be identified. See the guidance notes on clause 11.2(13).

The word "supply" is used to mean all the management and other non technical processes within the contract from the *starting date* to the *defects date*. This includes transport of the *goods* but does not just mean transport.

The word "deliver" has not been used. The defined term 'Delivery' is the state that applies when the conditions given in the definition of Delivery have been met. This is similar to "Completion" in other NEC contracts. See the guidance notes on clause 11.2(5)

There may be more than one Delivery and Delivery Date. See the guidance notes on clause 12.5.

Arrangement of the Supply Contract

The SC includes the following sections of text:

- the core clauses,
- the Option clauses,
- the Contract Data formats.

Other documents included in a contract when using the SC will include

- the Goods Information,
- the Supply Requirements (part of the Goods Information),
- the Price Schedule (once it has been completed and the Price agreed),
- documents resulting from choosing Options, such as the form of Performance Bond.

The successful tenderer's tender programme may also be incorporated as the Accepted Programme by reference in the Contract Data part two.

Subcontracts

The SC has been designed on the assumption that the *Supplier* may subcontract. In Appendix 4 of these guidance notes, guidance is given on how to convert the SC into a subcontract.

The NEC family includes several contracts that can be used for subcontracting. In a supply only arrangement they could be:

- the Professional Services Contract (PSC). To appoint a designer, who provides the service of designing all or part of the *goods* for the *Supplier*,
- the Supply Contract (SC),
- the Supply Short Contract (SSC).

These are all based upon similar principles to the SC and use common names and definitions. They have a small number of different provisions designed specifically for the different circumstances for which they should be used.

Because of the legal and practical problems of accountability which frequently ensue, no provision is made in the SC for nomination of subcontractors. The principle of the SC is that the *Supplier* is fully responsible for every aspect of managing the provision of the *goods* and *services*. Alternative strategies to nominating subcontractors whilst achieving similar objectives are as follows:

- providing for separate contracts, with the *Purchaser*'s *Supply Manager* managing the time and physical interfaces between them or
- to include the requirements for particular work to be subcontracted in the Goods Information.

Where national or international law requires, the Goods Information should include a statement of the award criteria for subcontracts.

Clause numbering

The core clauses in the SC are arranged in nine sections.

1 General
2 The *Supplier's* main responsibilities
3 Time
4 Testing and Defects
5 Payment
6 Compensation events
7 Title
8 Risks, liabilities, indemnities and insurance
9 Termination and dispute resolution

The first digit of a clause number is the number of the section to which the clause belongs. A clause may be subdivided, for example clause 16 includes four separate clauses numbered 16.1 to 16.4. Reference in these guidance notes to clause 16 is a reference to all the parts of the clause: reference to clause 16.1 is to that part only.

The Option clauses are numbered separately using a letter prefix. The prefix "X" is used for consistency with the other contracts in the NEC family. For Options that are specific to a country, the prefix "Y" is used followed by a further prefix to denote the country. For example Y (UK) which is applicable to the United Kingdom. Any additional clauses that are required for a specific purchase should be numbered with the prefix "Z".

Roles of the parties

The SC sets out the responsibilities and roles of the following parties

- the *Purchaser*,
- the *Supply Manager*,
- the *Supplier* and
- the *Adjudicator*.

The separate roles of *Purchaser*'s designer and *Supplier*'s designer are assumed but not mentioned in the contract.

The *Supply Manager*

The *Supply Manager* is appointed by the *Purchaser*, usually from his own staff, but may be from outside. His role within the SC is to manage the contract for the *Purchaser* with the intention of achieving the *Purchaser*'s objectives. The SC places considerable authority in the hands of the *Supply Manager*. It assumes that he has the *Purchaser*'s authority to carry out the actions and make the decisions which are required of him.

The contractual role of the *Supply Manager* is defined in terms of the actions and decisions he is to take. The *Supply Manager* is free to seek the *Purchaser*'s views as much or as little as his relationship and contract with the *Purchaser* requires. He will normally maintain close contact with the *Purchaser* so that his decisions reflect the *Purchaser*'s business objectives. He has authority to

- change the Goods Information, which includes the Supply Requirements that state amongst other things the destination of the *goods* (the delivery place),

- instruct the *Supplier*, and
- generally to apply his managerial judgement.

Positive management from both sides is therefore encouraged.

One important role of the *Supply Manager* is to monitor both the performance of the *Supplier* and the quality of the *goods* and *services*. He may take corrective action if either is not up to the standard required by the contract.

The *Adjudicator*

The *Adjudicator* is appointed jointly by the *Purchaser* and the *Supplier* for the contract. The method of selecting the *Adjudicator* may vary. Whichever method is chosen it is important that the person selected is acceptable to both parties and that he has the confidence of both Parties. One method is for the *Purchaser* to select a number of names and require the *Supplier* to choose one of them. Alternatively, the *Purchaser* may invite the *Supplier* to propose, suitable names from which the *Purchaser* selects one.

The *Adjudicator* becomes involved only when a dispute is referred to him. As a person independent of both Parties, he is required to give a decision on the dispute within stated time limits. If either Party does not accept his decision, they may proceed to the *tribunal* (usually either arbitration or the courts). Under the NEC Adjudicator's Contract, payment of the *Adjudicator*'s fee is shared equally by the Parties, unless agreed otherwise by the Parties.

The contract strategy

The *Purchaser* chooses the contract strategy. This should include consideration of whether the purchase is "stand alone" or part of a project. The choice of the Options to be incorporated into the contract is part of the contract strategy.

The *Purchaser* should take into account the following factors in deciding his contract strategy

- what the risks are and how they can be best managed,
- who is best placed to manage the risks,
- is the total risk tolerable for the *Supplier*,
- how clearly the Goods Information can be defined and
- the likelihood of change in the Goods Information (including the Supply Requirements).

The Options

The SC does not have main Options; the pricing mechanism is the Price Schedule (see below) which may include both lump sum and measured items, this means the financial risks are mainly carried by the *Supplier*.

There are ten Options prefixed "X", any of which may be incorporated in the contract according to particular circumstances and how it is considered that certain risks should be allocated. There are a few restrictions on use of some of the Options, which are explained in more detail later in these Guidance Notes.

The prefix numbers of the Options are common to the subject matter of that Option across all NEC contracts. Therefore there are gaps in the numbering of the Options where the subject matter is not appropriate to a supply contract.

The Options are

X1 Price adjustment for inflation
X2 Changes in the law
X3 Multiple currencies
X4 Parent company guarantee
X7 Delay damages
X12 Partnering
X13 Performance bond
X14 Advanced payment to the *Supplier*
X17 Low performance damages
X20 Key Performance Indicators (not used with Option X12)
Y(UK)1 Project Back Account
Y(UK)3 The Contract (Rights of Third Parties) Act 1999
Z *Additional conditions of contract*

It is not necessary to use any of these Options to form a contract; the chosen Option(s) must be identified in part one of the Contract Data.

The Price Schedule

The Price Schedule is a list of items which the *Supplier* is required to provide to meet the requirements of the Goods Information; this may involve descriptions of items of *goods, services* or the work activities which need to be done to Provide the Goods and Services. The Price Schedule may be prepared by the *Purchaser* or the *Supplier*, but it is always priced by the *Supplier*.

The *Supplier* prices the Price Schedule taking into account all the information in the contract documents and includes for all matters which are at the *Supplier*'s risk. A pro-forma Price Schedule is included at Appendix 5 in these Guidance Notes.

It is important that the *goods* and *services* to be supplied and any work activities to be provided by the *Supplier* are clearly described in the Price Schedule. The *Supplier* is then able to complete the Price Schedule and assess the rates and prices with reasonable confidence.

The pricing information in the Price Schedule is needed for assessing the amount due. The Prices are defined in clause 11.2(11). Payments for an item in the Price Schedule do not become due until the work described in the item has been completed unless a quantity and rate is stated in which case only the price for the quantity of work completed is included. Notes on payment are included in chapter 5 of these Guidance Notes.

CHAPTER 3   PROCEDURE FOR PREPARING A SUPPLY CONTRACT

Preparing the tender documents

The tender documents

Where the *Purchaser* intends to invite tenders from a number of suppliers, the tender documents are prepared by the *Purchaser*. These consist of

- Contract Data part one completed in full,
- Goods Information including the Supply Requirements,
- Contract Data part two prepared as a pro-forma for completion by each tenderer,
- Price Schedule (to be priced by each tenderer) and
- Form of Tender.

The *Purchaser* may also issue instructions to tenderers giving such details as how the tenders are to be assessed, advice on what is to be submitted, the date by which tenders are to be returned, the address for return and name of contact for enquiries regarding the tender.

Contract Data

In the clauses of the SC, the term Contract Data refers to the data that exists at the Contract Date. These are not necessarily those originally issued by the *Purchaser* (part one) or returned as part of the successful tenderer's offer (part two); they are sometimes changed during clarifications between the *Purchaser* and the potential *Supplier*.

The purpose of the Contract Data is to provide data as required by the *conditions of contract* specific to a particular contract. The terms in italics in the *conditions of contract* must be identified in the Contract Data in accordance with clause 11.1. The Contract Data is a key document in any contract in the NEC family.

Contract Data part one

This is completed by the *Purchaser* and consists of two parts; statements to be given in all contracts and optional statements. While many of the entries that are required are self evident when read with the relevant clauses, a worked example is given in Appendix 6 of these Guidance Notes.

Goods Information

The documents containing the Goods Information provided by the *Purchaser* are identified in part one of the Contract Data. Any Goods Information for the *Supplier*'s design submitted by tenderers with their tender is to be identified in part two of the Contract Data.

Most of the Goods Information will be in the form of a specification and drawings describing in detail the *goods* and *services* which is to be provided by the *Supplier*. The Goods Information should be drafted with great care. Where information is provided by non-documentary means such as models, they should be identified and their availability and location stated.

There are several references to the Goods Information in the *conditions of contract* and users should also refer to Chapter 4 of these Guidance Notes the "Supply Requirements" as they apply to and are included in the Goods Information.

The Goods Information should include the following items as they may apply to a particular contract. The related clause numbers are given in brackets.

Description of the *goods* and *services*: (11.2(8))

- Description (detailed as necessary) of the *goods* and *services*, including specifications of the plant and materials, drawings and information about the environment where the *goods* and *services* are to be put to use.

- Any constraints on how the *Supplier* is to provide the *goods* and *services*, both at the delivery place and where the *goods* and *services* are to be put to use e.g. restrictions on access, hours of working, and sequences of work.

The degree of detail and definition in the Goods Information is a key decision that the *Purchaser* should make and in doing so he should consider:

- Design requirements,
- Materials and workmanship performance,
- Specification for replacement parts and spares,
- Requirements for supply and storage before use,
- Essential functional requirements to administer the contract (eg: communications, risk management, procurement and quality management).

Provision of spares.

If the *Supplier* is to provide the *Purchaser* with any spares and replacement parts for the *goods* these should be stated in the Goods Information. The spares may be those necessary for the operation and maintenance of the *goods*, therefore both routine and strategic spares are included. The SC does not include for the *Supplier* to provide spares after the last *defects date*; if the *Purchaser* requires spares after this date he should make separate arrangements with the *Supplier* using, for example the SSC.

Delivery (11.2(5))
The work required to be done by the Delivery Date to supply the *goods* and *services*, which could include a statement, in the form of a list, of work that can remain undone at the Delivery Date.

Supplier's design
(21.1). A statement of those parts of the *goods* and *services* which the *Supplier* is to design. The form of this statement will depend on the extent of the *Supplier*'s design responsibility. This could be:

- The design performance criteria and design life the *Supplier* is required to meet.
- A list of what design the *Supplier* is left to do.
- A list of what design the *Purchaser* has done with the *Supplier* being made responsible for designing the remainder.
- A detailed and prescribed design that the *Supplier* is required to do or meet.

(21.2). The procedures which the *Supplier* is to follow in carrying his design should be stated including particulars of the design which are to be submitted to the *Supply Manager* such as requirements for certification and/or checking.

Using the *Supplier*'s design and services (22.1)
The purposes for which the *Purchaser* may require to use and copy the *Supplier*'s design and services, or any restriction on use and copying, that differs from any purpose connected with the use or alteration of the *goods* and *services*.

Services and other things (23.2)
Any services and other things to be provided by the *Purchaser* for the use of the *Supplier*. Similarly any services to be provided by the *Supplier* for the use of the *Purchaser* and others whilst carrying out the supply of the *goods* and *services*.

Subcontracting (24)
Lists of elements which the *Purchaser* expects to be subcontracted; statement of any elements that should not be subcontracted; any specific elements that must be subcontracted.

Health and safety [25.4]. The particular health and safety requirements such as the safety regulations for the *goods* and *services*. Any health and safety plan as may be required by law should also be included.

Programme (31.2). See the explanatory notes on this clause in chapter 5.

Tests and inspections

(40.1). Description of tests and inspections to be carried out by the *Supplier*, the *Supply Manager* and others.

(40.2). Details of which records, data sheets, materials, facilities and samples for tests and inspections are to be provided by the *Supplier* and which are to be provided by the *Purchaser*.

(41.1). Details of any testing or inspection which is to be carried out before Delivery, together with details of the test or inspection.

Title (71.1). Details of the requirements for marking the *goods* before Delivery.

Parent company guarantee (X4.1). Details of the form of guarantee required by the *Purchaser*.

Performance bond (X13.1). Details of the form of bond required by the *Purchaser*.

Advanced payment bond (X14.2). Details of the advanced payment bond required by the *Purchaser*.

While it is likely most users will have their own form of bond, some revision may be necessary to align them with the terminology used in the SC.

Contract Data part two

As for Contract Data part one, entries are in two parts, namely those statements given in all contracts and optional statements.

The *percentage for overheads and profit* is the figure entered by the tenderer to represent broadly the *Supplier*'s overheads and profit in respect of the *Supplier*'s own work and any subcontracted work. The level of the percentage is an important factor in assessing the financial aspect of a tender.

The *price schedule* entry will be a reference to another document (see Appendix 6).

The tendered total of the Prices will be the figure transferred from the total of the Prices column of the Price Schedule.

Four optional statements follow, from which the *Purchaser* will have selected those he requires. For instance, the fourth optional statement regarding the *delivery date* should be included only if the *Purchaser* has not stated the *delivery date* in the Contract Data part one and wishes tenderers to submit their proposals.

The first optional statement applies if the tenderers are required to submit design proposals. The reference in this entry will be to separate documents which show this design.

The second optional statement applies where the *Supplier* may wish to restrict access to certain areas of his work for business or commercial reasons. The *Supplier* should not restrict access to the *Supply Manager* which he requires to undertake his duties in the contract.

The third optional statement applies where tenderers are required to submit with their tenders a programme for the supply of the *goods* and *services*. The reference in this entry will be to a separate document.

The Price Schedule

Entries in the first four columns of the Price Schedule (see Appendix 5) are made either by the *Purchaser* or the tendering supplier. In some cases where the *Purchaser* enters the items, he may invite tenderers to insert any additional items which they consider necessary. The entries may also be the result of clarifications. There are no standard rules for determining the items to be inserted, but where the tendering supplier prepares the items in the Price Schedule, the *Purchaser* may choose to specify criteria or guidelines. The last two columns are always completed by the tenderer since these prices comprise a fundamental part of his offer. It is important that the items in the Price Schedule comply with and are consistent with the *Supplier*'s programme.

The pricing of items are of two kinds.

- Lump sum items, in which the amount entered in the Price column covers the amount for the *goods* and *services* or the work described. This is the amount paid to the *Supplier* when the *goods* and *services* are supplied or the item of work described has been completed.
- Quantity-related items, in which the quantity is entered in the fourth column and the rate per unit quantity is entered in the fifth column by the tenderer. The quantity is multiplied by the rate to give an amount in the Price column. The *Supplier* is paid for the actual quantity done in accordance with the contract. This may be different from the original quantity entered against the item in the Price Schedule as a result of errors in the original quantity, refinement of the calculation of the quantity or other reason. This process is called re-measurement, or sometimes ad-measurement.

Pricing of the Price Schedule should cover all the work required to comply with the Goods Information. The total of the Prices is the payment to be made to the *Supplier* for the work done by the *Supplier* in the supply of the *goods* and *services* described in the Goods Information, but subject to re-measurement.

The *Supplier* may be paid after different periods of time; say at the end of each calendar month, the total number of months is entered in the Quantity column. The amount per month for carrying out the work described in the Description column is entered in the Rate column. The total amount to be paid to the *Supplier* for providing the *goods* and *services* described throughout the contract is calculated from the number of time periods multiplied by the rate per period.

Inviting tenders

It is common practice to issue instructions to tenderers. These instructions do not become part of the contract documents as they are intended merely to give guidance to those tendering. For example, the *Purchaser* may wish tendering suppliers to submit information about how they are proposing to supply the *goods* and *services*. If so, the *Supplier*'s programme submitted with the tender is included in part two of the Contract Data. When a tender is accepted, the programme becomes the first Accepted Programme.

The instructions to tenderers should also state which management functions are to be performed by the people to be identified in the Contract Data.

A complete form of tender should be submitted, comprising the *Supplier*'s formal offer to Provide the Goods and Services. A sample form for this purpose is given in Appendix 2.

Preparing a tender

Preparing a tender will consist of completing the entries in part two of the Contract Data and completing and pricing the Price Schedule. For both of these a thorough understanding of the *conditions of contract* is essential. The tenderer should also be clear on the nature of the *goods* and *services* to be provided by the *Supplier* as detailed in the Goods Information and other contract documents.

Assessing tenders

To ensure equal treatment of all tenderers and to assist in their under-standing of the *Purchaser*'s requirements, the criteria upon which tenders are to be assessed and the weight given to various factors should be clearly stated in the instructions to tenderers. These criteria may include the proposals for the contract. It is important that all documents submitted with tenders are carefully examined, as once accepted a tender becomes contractually binding on both Parties. This particularly applies to the *Supplier*'s programme if submitted as part of the tender. A number of compensation events refer to dates on the *Supplier*'s programme. Thus careful examination by the *Purchaser* of these dates and their effects is essential.

Creating the contract

Frequently, discussions with one or more tenderers are necessary to clarify intentions, to agree amendments, to eliminate qualifications which are not acceptable to the *Purchaser* and to discuss the *Supplier*'s programme. It is important to minimise these discussions since extended discussions can result in abuse of the tendering process. This can be achieved by careful preparation of tender documents and instructions to tenderers and by stating award criteria in objective terms.

The creation of a contract can be by means of acceptance of a tender or a revised tender or by means of acceptance by the *Supplier* of a counter-offer prepared by or on behalf of the *Purchaser*. A binding contract is thus created, although some purchasers may require such acceptance being subject to a formal agreement. A suitable form of agreement is included in Appendix 3, but purchasers often have their own standard forms. Essentially, they record the agreement between the two Parties and identify the documents which make up the contract.

CHAPTER 4   SUPPLY REQUIREMENTS

Introduction

All NEC contracts make use of a reference to "Information" in which the buying party sets out what the supplying party is to do. The obligation to work in accordance with that information is then set down in the *conditions of contract*. In order to maintain this continuity across the NEC family, clause 20.1 in the SC states, "The *Supplier* Provides the Goods and Services in accordance with the Goods Information". The Goods Information likewise is defined as information which specifies and describes the *goods* and *services* and states any constraints on how the *Supplier* Provides the Goods and Services.

In any supply contract the information which states the *Purchaser*'s requirements for the management of the supply (including transport) of the *goods* that clarifies how actions, costs and risks are allocated between the buyer and seller in respect of these processes is important because the parties to these contracts may never meet directly. This is especially the case in international transactions and in any case this information relates to the processes in the transaction, not to the description of the *goods* themselves.

This information is provided in the SC as Supply Requirements which is defined in clause 11.2(16).

The Supply Requirements although defined separately for the reasons stated above are by virtue of the definition of Goods Information, a constraint on how the *Supplier* Provides the Goods and Services and therefore part of the Goods Information. See clause 11.2(8).

The SC requires users to prescribe their Supply Requirements separately to ensure the matters set out above are dealt with clearly. Users may, if necessary, make use of Incoterms[1] to do this. Incoterms are the official rules for the interpretation of trade terms that are most commonly used in foreign trade. They are designed to overcome the uncertainties of different interpretations of trading terms in different countries. Incoterms may apply to a contract of sale (supply contract) but not a contract for carriage and moreover they only apply in very distinct respects. Incoterms are therefore not in themselves a contract and only cover some of the obligations required by a supply contract.

For domestic procurement or international procurement within common trading areas, users may prefer to make their own arrangements as they are unlikely to involve freight forwarding agents and customs barriers. However many of the functions, risks and costs addressed in Incoterms may still apply or can at least be used as a guide for consideration by the Parties.

Preparing the Supply Requirements

The principal decisions to be made by the *Purchaser* when preparing the Supply Requirements are:

- What are the requirements for the management of the supply of the *goods*,
- To what extent does he wish the *Supplier* to move the *goods*,
- By what mode of transport,
- To where (the delivery place),
- What information is to be provided by the *Supplier* in relation to the supply management and transport and
- What are the requirements of the Customs authorities for export and import.

---

[1] International Chamber of Commerce, Incoterms 2000, Paris, January 2000.

The Supply Requirements should contain complete statements of how the *Purchaser* requires the *goods* be transported from the *Supplier* to the *Purchaser*, which Party carries out specified actions in connection with the supply, the information to be provided by the *Supplier* in order to comply with Delivery, and any other matter or information which the *Purchaser* requires in connection with supply of the *goods*.

Example Supply Requirements

The following schedule is provided as an example:

1. The requirements for the supply are	[State the constraints on how the *Supplier* manufactures, prototypes, tests and stores the *goods* including order and timing]
2. The requirements for transport are	[State the extent to which the *Supplier* transports the *goods* and the mode of transport]
3. The delivery place is	[State the location where the *goods* are to be placed by the *Supplier*, such as whether it is a dispatch department at the *Supplier*'s premises, the *Purchaser* is to collect or other location the *Purchaser* may require. If the delivery place for the *services* is different to the *goods* state it here]

4. Actions of the Parties during supply	Action	Party who does it
	Giving notice of Delivery	
	Checking packing and marking before dispatch	
	Contracting for transport	
	Pay costs of transport	
	Arrange access to delivery place	
	Loading the *goods*	
	Unloading the *goods*	
For international procurement	Undertake export requirements	
	Undertake import requirements	

5. Information to be provided by the *Supplier*	Title of document
	Packing lists for cases and their contents
	Copy of invoice for the *goods*
	Delivery Note
	Test results and maintenance manuals
For international procurement	Licences, authorisations and other formalities associated with export of the *goods*
	Air waybill or Bill of Landing with associated landing, delivery and forwarding order
	The Bill of entry endorsed by the importation authority
	Customs work sheets, showing tax, duties and surcharges which the law of the country into which the *goods* are being imported requires the importer to pay
	Invoice from the importation clearing agent showing airline fees, landing charges, wharfage and dock dues
	Specify other import documents required by authorised officials

All other information not pertinent to the above is given in the balance of the Goods Information.

Preparing Supply Requirements when using Incoterms

If users select to use Incoterms in the preparation of the Supply Requirements the information requirements set out above are given categories and terms from Incoterms and the *Purchaser* may prepare his Supply Requirements by selecting the category and term he requires and state the delivery place. (See table below).

Group	Category	Term	Delivery Place
E	departure	EXW	
F	main carriage unpaid	FCA, FAS, FOB	
C	main carriage paid	CFR, CIF, CPT, CIP	
D	arrival	DAF, DES, DEQ, DDU, DDP	

For example the Supply Requirements could state:

"EXW – Incoterms 2000. The *Supplier*'s factory in Birmingham, England" **or** "DDP – Incoterms 2000. The *Purchaser*'s store in Kathmandu, Nepal".

By doing so, the Parties obligations described in Incoterms for the category and term selected are now incorporated into the contract as part of the Supply Requirements and hence the Goods Information.

The obligations of seller and buyer for the selected Incoterm determine each Party's costs, risks and insurance requirements incidental to the supply and transport of the *goods* from *Supplier* to *Purchaser*.

For each of the thirteen terms, Incoterms set out obligations of the seller (the *Supplier*) in ten paragraphs identified as A1 to A10 and the corresponding obligations of the buyer (the *Purchaser*) in paragraphs B1 to B10. These obligations cover the following subjects:

A	The *Supplier*'s obligations	B	The *Purchaser*'s obligations
A1	Provision of goods in conformity with contract	B1	Payment of the price
A2	Licences, authorisations and formalities	B2	Licences, authorisations and formalities
A3	Contracts of carriage and insurance	B3	Contracts of carriage and insurance
A4	Delivery	B4	Taking delivery
A5	Transfer of risks	B5	Transfer of risks
A6	Division of costs	B6	Division of costs
A7	Notice to the buyer	B7	Notice to the seller
A8	Proof of delivery, transport document or equivalent electronic message	B8	Proof of delivery, transport document or equivalent electronic message
A9	Checking – packing – marking	B9	Inspection of goods
A10	Other obligations	B10	Other obligations

When preparing the Supply Requirements and other parts of the Goods Information, there is no need to repeat what is already stated in the above listed obligations, because they are brought into the contract by quoting which Incoterm applies. Users should take careful note of paragraph 10 "The expression No obligation" in Incoterms 2000.

However, Incoterms obligations are drafted quite generically and in some cases users may find the need to be more specific or even change them. For example if the *goods* are to be supplied EXW, the *Supplier* is not required to load the *goods* onto any vehicle which the *Purchaser* sends to collect them. If the *Purchaser* does require the *Supplier* to load the *goods*, this must be stated clearly in the Supply Requirements as an obligation in addition to that required by the term; the passing of risk is amended as well. Before attempting to change an Incoterm obligation or add any information users should take careful note of paragraph 11 'Variants of Incoterms' in Incoterms 2000.

Information to be provided by the *Supplier* with the *goods* when they are transported may also be a matter which requires particular attention. Term A8

(Proof of delivery, transport document or equivalent electronic message) does make reference to such information but additional documentation or prescription may be required in certain circumstances.

While Incoterms are designed to regulate internationally the trading conventions of how the functions, costs and risks are split between buyer and seller in the transport and supply of *goods*, the SC, being the contract of sale contractually regulates these functions, costs and risks between the *Purchaser* and *Supplier*. When incorporating Incoterms into the SC users need to be aware of and manage any potential differences between the two.

For example term A4 states that for delivery (to take place) the seller must place the goods at the disposal of the buyer at the named place of delivery. The SC does not use the word "delivery" it defines Delivery in clause 11.2(5) as follows:

Delivery is when the *Supplier* has

- done all the work which the Goods Information states he is to do by the Delivery Date and
- corrected Defects which would have prevented the *Purchaser* from using the *goods* and *services* or Others from doing their work.

The Goods Information may require tasks other than mere transport from one place to another to be performed before Delivery. Such tasks could include passing of tests in the *Supplier*'s factory, inspection before transport, labelling to comply with title provisions before payment is made and provision of specified documentation.

The term A1 requires "The seller must provide the *goods* and a commercial invoice, or its equivalent electronic message, in conformity with the contract of sale and any other evidence of conformity which may be required by the contract". It could be concluded that Delivery as defined in the SC has to be satisfied for the delivery obligation in Incoterms to have taken place. The importance of this must be appreciated because the transfer of risk takes place on delivery in the Incoterms and on Delivery in the SC.

Another matter users should consider carefully is insurance. Incoterms refer mainly to insurance of the goods in transit whereas the SC requires insurance cover, to be effected by either party, for the *Supplier*'s risks assessed from the combination of clauses 80.1 and 81.1.

Example Supply Requirements incorporating Incoterms

The following schedule is provided as an example.

In this example a *Supplier* in Japan is required by a *Purchaser* in South Africa to ship the *goods* to the Port of Durban where the *Purchaser* has arranged to offload the *goods*, clear customs and transport them to his own place of storage before putting them into use.

The *Supplier* transports and supplies the *goods* in accordance with Incoterms 2000.

Group	Category	Term	Delivery Place
D	arrival	DDU	Port of Durban – South Africa

The Supplier's obligations are A1–A10 supplemented (for example) with the following additional requirements (if any).

	Supplier's Obligation	Additional requirements
A3	Contracts of carriage and insurance	The Supplier contracts for carriage with … [State the transport company].
A7	Notice to the buyer	"Sufficient notice" of the dispatch of the goods means not less than 7 days.
A8	Proof of delivery, transport document or equivalent electronic message	In addition to the documentation stated; The Supplier provides the following documents: [State the documents]
A10	Other obligations	The Supplier provides a statement certifying that all goods are lead free.

All other information not pertinent to the above 10 sets of obligations is given in the balance of the Goods Information.

It is assumed that users incorporating Incoterms are familiar with their application as it is beyond the scope of these Guidance Notes to provide any further explanation or guidance on them. Users should acquaint themselves with the Incoterms if they intend to use them to create their Supply Requirements.

1 General

CORE CLAUSES

Actions 10

10.1   The first statement in this clause obliges the *Purchaser*, the *Supplier* and the *Supply Manager* to do everything which the contract states they are to do. It is the only clause which uses the future tense. For simplicity, everything else is in the present tense. Where actions are permitted but not obligatory, the term 'may' is used.

The other statement specifies how the parties are to act. This is a fundamental requirement of all contracts in the NEC family and is designed to encourage a collaborative rather than a confrontational approach to management of the contract.

Identified and 11
defined terms 11.1   The main definitions used in the contract are given in clause 11. Other definitions are given in optional clauses where they are specific to a particular Option. The conventions for italics and capital initials as used in the SC are also used in this section of the guidance notes.

11.2   (1) The contract requires the *Supplier* to submit to the *Supply Manager* a programme of how he intends to supply the *goods* and *services*. The *Supply Manager* either accepts or rejects (with reasons) the programme. This programme must be regularly updated – see clause 32.2. The latest programme becomes the Accepted Programme when it is accepted by the *Supply Manager*. Therefore the Accepted Programme will change during the course of the contract.

The definition of the Accepted Programme allows for the two situations where there may or may not have been a requirement for the *Supplier* to submit a programme with his tender. If a tender programme is identified in part two of the Contract Data it becomes the first Accepted Programme when the contract comes into existence. If a tender programme is intended to become the Accepted Programme, it should conform to the requirements of clause 31.2.

(2) The Contract Date is used to define the date when the contract comes into existence, regardless of the means by which this is achieved.

(3) The word Defect has the meaning set out in the contract. Any part of the *goods* and *services* which is not in accordance with

- the Goods Information,
- the *Supplier*'s design which has been accepted by the *Supply Manager*, or
- the applicable law

is a Defect.

(4) This definition of Defined Cost, which is used in the assessment of compensation events, includes four basic components. Defined Cost is the cost of the components listed for work done by the *Supplier* and his Subcontractors. The *Purchaser* is protected against artificially inflated amounts for any of these components by clause 52.1. This requires any amounts included in Defined Cost to be at open market or competitively

tendered levels. The cost of preparing quotations for compensation events is specifically excluded.

(5) The Goods Information should state what work is to be done to achieve Delivery; disputes can arise if this is not done clearly and unambiguously. This provides flexibility for the *Purchaser* to specify Delivery at the level he requires and avoids the uncertainty associated with terms such as "substantial" or "partial". Delivery is therefore a defined state and not a date. It is when the *Supply Manager* decides the *Supplier* has met all requirements in the Goods Information for Delivery.

The *Purchaser* should consider carefully how he wants to define when Delivery is achieved and put that in the Goods Information. He should also state what documentation the *Supplier* is to provide before Delivery is achieved.

(6) The *delivery date* is stated in the Contract Data (either in part one or part two). It may be changed in various ways under the SC, for example as a consequence of a compensation event or of an agreement to accelerate.

The Delivery Date is the date by which the *Supplier* is contractually obliged to achieve Delivery of the *goods* and *services* – clause 30.1. There may be more than one Delivery and Delivery Date; see clause 12.5.

(8) Goods Information is information which specifies what *goods* and *services* the *Supplier* is to provide. It can be in the form of a specification and drawings. The Goods Information also sets out any constraints on how the *Supplier* Provides the Goods and Services. Further advice on the contents of Goods Information is given under "Preparing the Tender Documents" earlier in these Guidance Notes.

Goods Information may be provided by the *Supplier*, if it relates to the *Supplier*'s design. Only the *Supply Manager* may change the Goods Information – see clause 14.3.

(9) The term 'Others' provides a convenient means of reference to people and organisations not directly involved in the contract.

(11) The Prices are the basis on which the amount due is calculated and may comprise both lump sums and quantified items. See the notes on clause 50.2.

(12) The *price schedule* is priced by the Supplier at tender stage and includes the Prices for all of the *goods* and *services* required by the Goods Information. The *price schedule* in the contract may change, for example to take account of compensation events. Therefore the term Price Schedule is used throughout the contract, which will be the *price schedule*, unless it is changed in accordance with the contract.

(13) The definition of "To Provide the Goods and Services" in conjunction with the definition of Goods Information 11.2(8) identifies the *Supplier*'s main obligation in clause 20.1.

(14) The Risk Register provides a means of identifying risk at the beginning of the contract and then managing it throughout the period of the contract. The number and type of risks will vary and will depend on many factors, such as nature of the *goods* and *services*, where the *goods* are manufactured and supplied to, and changes in the Goods Information.

At tender stage each Party lists in the Contract Data Parts one and two those risks that they wish to see included in the Risk Register. Once the contract is awarded the *Supply Manager*, with the assistance of the *Supplier*, should draw up the first Risk Register, setting out the risks and the actions to be taken to manage them.

The Risk Register is a constantly evolving document. New risks are added as soon as they are identified and existing risks are removed once they have passed. This process is managed through the early warning system – clause 16.

It is important to note that the Risk Register deals only with the management of risks and not their allocation, which is set out in the rest of the contract. Therefore neither Party is taking responsibility for a risk when they list it in the Contract Data or when they notify the risk later.

(15) The definition of Subcontractor excludes a supplier of plant and materials to the *Supplier*, unless those plant and materials were wholly or partly designed specifically for the *goods*.

(16) The Supply Requirements is information which states the *Supplier*'s obligations for the supply including transport of the *goods*. The Supply Requirements are an important part of the Goods Information (see clause 11.2(8)). Also see chapter 4 "The Supply Requirements" of these Guidance Notes.

Interpretation and the law 12

12.5 This clause allows for multiple Delivery and hence the respective Delivery Date. The Delivery Date will be stated in the Contract Data for the *goods* and *services* either as a single *delivery date* for the whole of the *goods* and *services* or as a schedule of *delivery dates* for parts of the *goods* and *services* as identified in the Contract Data. For example the *services* may be required on a regular basis and are finished with the *goods* by one Delivery Date, or it may be appropriate to state another Delivery Date for the *services* which are finished following the Delivery of the *goods*.

The *defects date* is stated in the Contract Data as a period of time after Delivery. Hence each Delivery will have it's own *defects date*.

Communications 13

13.1 The phrase 'in a form which can be read, copied and recorded' includes a document sent by post, cable, electronic mail, facsimile transmission, telex, and on disc, magnetic tape or other electronic means. It does not, however include oral communications.

13.3 This clause together with clause 13.4 establishes the use of a *period for reply*, (identified in the Contract Data part one) which is the period that either Party has to provide any reply wherever the term is used in the *conditions of contract*.

If different periods of reply are needed, such as when responding to details of a design provided by the *Supplier*, it may be appropriate to state a particular *period for reply* in the Contract Data.

13.5 This clause provides for extending the *period for reply* by agreement between the *Supply Manager* and the *Supplier*.

13.7 The requirement to notify information required by the contract separately is intended to avoid important things being overlooked if they are "hidden" within other routine communications. Requiring separate notices also makes it easier to track the procedure following the issue of a notice.

13.8 The SC contains a number of examples of situations in which the *Supply Manager* must either accept or reject a document which contains proposals submitted by the *Supplier*. In each such case, grounds for rejecting the submission are stated. This does not prevent the *Supply Manager* from rejecting the submission for other reasons, but if he does so, the rejection is a compensation event (clause 60.1(8)). This arrangement limits the *Supplier*'s risk and provides more objective criteria on which to judge acceptance.

The Supply Manager 14 The *Supply Manager* is the key person involved in the management of the contract from the *Purchaser*'s point of view. His duties and authority are described in the clauses of the contract. They are not summarised in a single clause. It is assumed that the *Supply Manager* will confer with the *Purchaser* as necessary, in deciding which of various actions to take and in making other decisions which affect the outcome of the contract. For the purposes of the contract almost all dealings with the *Supplier* are handled by the *Supply*

Manager. If the *Supply Manager* needs to consult the *Purchaser*, the internal arrangements between them should be such that the contractual time limits can be achieved.

14.1 The SC contains a number of examples of situations in which the *Supply Manager* must either accept or reject a submission made by the *Supplier*. In carrying out this function it is not intended that the *Supply Manager* should act as the *Supplier's* quality checker and pick up errors or mistakes.

This clause makes it clear that even if the *Supply Manager* fails to spot such an error the *Supplier* remains responsible for all of the information he provides and ensuring that it complies with the contract. The *Supply Manager's* acceptance does not change that responsibility.

14.2 On major supply contracts, or on projects which involve many major items for purchase, it is normal for the *Supply Manager* to have staff to help him to carry out his duties. This clause enables him to delegate specific duties and authorities under the contract to particular people. For example the *Supply Manager* may notify the *Supplier* who is authorised to receive the *goods* and sign the delivery note if one is required by the Goods Information.

Delegation of particular duties or authorities does not prevent the *Supply Manager* from also acting himself and does not change the *Supply Manager's* responsibility for these duties.

All such delegations only take affect once the *Supply Manager* has notified the *Supplier* of them, in a notification that complies with clauses 13.1 and 13.7.

14.3 This clause gives the *Supply Manager* a wide power to change the Goods Information provided by either Party. The SC does not limit the ordinary meaning of the word "change". Consequently, an instruction under this clause may be an addition to or deletion of part of the Goods Information as well as alterations to it. All such changes are potentially compensation events as set out in clause 60.1(1).

Disclosure 15

15.1 This clause obligates the *Purchaser*, the *Supplier* and the *Supply Manager* acting on the *Purchaser's* behalf not to disclose any information except as necessary to carry out their duties under the contract. This is particularly important in regard to security or commercially sensitive information.

Early warning 16 The purpose of this clause is to oblige the Parties to work together to warn any possible problems before they occur, so that they can be avoided or their effects mitigated.

16.1 This clause requires the *Supply Manager* and the *Supplier* to notify each other as soon as they are aware of any matter which could

- increase the total of the Prices,
- delay Delivery,
- impair the performance of the *goods* in use or
- impair the usefulness of the *services* to the *Purchaser*.

The *Supply Manager* and *Supplier* are motivated to give early warning in order to maximise the time available to consider the problem and thereby to increase the likelihood of finding the best solution.

The sanction for failure by the *Supplier* to give early warning in these circumstances is to reduce payment due to him for a related compensation event (clause 63.6).

In addition the *Supplier* may, if he wishes, give an early warning of any other matter that could increase his total cost. This will not, in itself, lead to any additional payment to the *Supplier* unless the event is a compensation event.

As soon as an early warning is given, the *Supply Manager* should start the management process by entering the matter into the Risk Register.

16.2   This clause authorises the *Supply Manager* or *Supplier* to call a risk reduction meeting at any time to discuss problems or potential problems of which notice has been given so that they can be considered.

         If required, any other people who could assist in solving the problem or mitigating it's effects should be required by either Party to attend the meeting. These may include Subcontractors or suppliers, or representatives of the *Purchaser.*

16.3   This clause provides the items for the agenda of the risk reduction meeting. Those attending are required to co-operate in solving the problem irrespective of where the contractual responsibility may rest. The procedure set out in this clause gives priority to dealing with the problem rather than to contractual responsibility which is dealt with by other provisions in the contract.

         The final bullet point of the action list allows those attending to discuss and agree what risks have now passed such that they can be removed from the Risk Register. This enables the Risk Register to be kept up to date and manageable.

16.4   The decisions made at a risk reduction meeting are recorded by the *Supply Manager* on the Risk Register.

Ambiguities and **17**
inconsistencies 17.1   This clause is intended to ensure that action is taken as soon as possible to deal with ambiguities and inconsistencies noticed in the contract documents. There is no stated precedence of documents. The *Supply Manager* has the responsibility of resolving the ambiguity or inconsistency in the documents.

         An instruction to change the Goods Information to resolve an ambiguity or inconsistency is a compensation event provided it is covered by clause 60.1(1). When assessing the effect this compensation event has upon time and money the interpretation most favourable to the Party which did not provide the Goods Information that was changed will be used (clause 63.9).

Illegal and impossible **18**
requirements 18.1   A change to the Goods Information in order to resolve illegal or impossible requirements in the Goods Information is a compensation event (clause 60.1(1)).

Prevention **19**
         19.1   This is in effect a "force majeure" clause; however it is limited to an event during the transport of the *goods* to the Delivery Place. It covers events that either stop the *Supplier* from achieving Delivery or make it impossible for him to achieve Delivery on time, whatever measures he might take.

         A delay to planned Delivery which can (as opposed to will) be recovered by acceleration, by increased resources or by adjusting the programme does not stop the *Supplier* from supplying on time. The *Supplier* must demonstrate that there is no reasonable means by which he can supply the *goods* on time for the event to be recognised under the second bullet point.

         Once an event is notified or otherwise known to the *Supply Manager* and it is accepted that the criteria for the event have been met, the *Supply Manager* has authority to manage the consequences in the best interests of the *Purchaser.* The *Supply Manager* could, for example, instruct a re-ordering of the programme or even change the design. The event is a compensation event (60.1(15)) and therefore at the *Purchaser's* risk for both time and cost.

         In certain circumstances the event may lead to termination by the *Purchaser* – see clause 91.7.

2 The *Supplier*'s main responsibilities

CORE CLAUSES

The clauses in this section sets out the *Supplier*'s main responsibilities. Other sections deal with particular responsibilities appropriate to the section heading.

Providing the Goods and Services **20**

20.1   This clause states the *Supplier*'s basic obligation. The term Provide the Goods and Services is defined in clause 11.2(13). It includes providing all the necessary resources to achieve the end result. The Goods Information provided by the *Purchaser* should state everything the *Supplier* is to do and state those parts which the *Purchaser* designs.

The *Supplier*'s design **21**

The SC is suitable for use where the design is done wholly or partly by either the *Purchaser* or the *Supplier*. In supply contracts it is common for the bulk of the design to be done by the *Supplier* however between these two limits it is likely that the contract will include some design done by or on behalf of the *Purchaser.*

21.1   Those parts of the *goods* which the *Purchaser* designs should be stated in the Goods Information provided by the *Purchaser* and the interfaces with those parts of the *goods* designed by the *Supplier* identified. This may be done by stating 'everything except the following' or 'the following'. It is not recommended that parts of an element of goods should be designed by different parties as this may confuse liability in the event of Defects occurring.

Where the *Supplier* is required to design a part of the *goods*, the *Purchaser* should state in the Goods Information the criteria to which he requires designs to conform. This may include details of the form, geometry and dimensions of the *goods*, specifications, codes of practice, standards and environmental criteria. (See earlier notes on 'Preparing the tender documents'.)

Where the *Supplier* is to carry out most of the design, similar criteria may be stated in the form of a performance specification. This will describe the characteristics, nature and performance of the finished *goods* and should include any limitations which the *Purchaser* wishes to impose upon appearance, durability, operating and maintenance cost, etc. Any change to the allocation of design responsibility or change or addition to the design criteria in the Goods Information constitutes a change to the Goods Information and is a compensation event.

21.2   The procedures for submission by the *Supplier* of design particulars and acceptance by the *Supply Manager* are set out in this clause. The time limits are those stated in clause 13. They are intended to encourage prompt action by the parties so that delay can be avoided and the whole process properly managed.

Two reasons for not accepting the *Supplier*'s design are stated. The *Supply Manager* is not obliged to refuse acceptance of the *Supplier*'s design which does not comply with the Goods Information but, if he does accept such design, he should change the Goods Information accordingly. As stated in clause 60.1(1), such a change to the Goods Information may or may not be a compensation event (see explanatory notes on clause 60.1(1)).

Sometimes the *Supply Manager* will see in the design submitted by the *Supplier* characteristics which, if they had been foreseen, he would earlier have stated to have been unacceptable by including an appropriate constraint in the Goods Information. In this situation, the *Supply Manager* should add the constraint to

the Goods Information in order to justify his withholding of acceptance of the *Supplier*'s design. This change to the Goods Information is a compensation event. This clause in the SC ensures that the *Supplier* is protected from the risk of additional constraints on his design being introduced after his commitment to the Prices for the *goods* and *services* has been made.

Clause 14.1 makes clear that, when the *Supply Manager* accepts the *Supplier*'s design, there is no change of liability for the design. The *Purchaser* is thus placing reliance on the design skill of the *Supplier*.

The final sentence is intended to prevent abortive work which would result if the *Supplier* began to manufacture to a design which had not been accepted.

21.3 It is important that design submissions by the *Supplier* are in packages which are capable of being properly assessed, without reliance on information that has not at that time been provided.

Using the *Supplier*'s design and *services* 22

22.1 The rights over drawings, documents, design and the like prepared by the *Supplier* for the contract would normally remain with the *Supplier*. This clause, unless otherwise stated in the Goods Information, gives the *Purchaser* an entitlement to use the design, software, drawings and documents for the purposes stated.

Working with the *Purchaser* and Others 23

23.1 The *Supplier*'s duty to co-operate with Others is expressed in general terms only – the detailed requirements will depend on the particular circumstances of the *goods* and *services* being provided and where they are to be provided to. Where the *Supplier*'s obligations may affect or interfere with the activities of the *Purchaser* or Others, it is important that interfaces in respect of location and timing are agreed by all parties and shown on the *Supplier*'s programme.

The exchange of information about the *goods* and *services* is important, especially when it relates to health and safety matters, where it may be required in order to comply with the law as well as with the contract.

23.2 This clause states the obligations of the Parties to provide services and other things. Details of all such requirements should be included in the Goods Information. Failure by the *Supplier* to fulfil his obligations in this respect will lead to him paying the additional costs (if any) that the *Purchaser* incurs as a result of that failure.

Failure by the *Purchaser* to fulfil his obligations in this respect may result in a compensation event under clause 60.1(3).

Subcontracting 24

This clause applies only to Subcontractors, as defined by clause 11.2(15). It does not apply to other suppliers that the *Supplier* may appoint that do not fall within this definition.

24.1 This clause makes it clear that if the *Supplier* subcontracts any of his work he, and not the Subcontractor, remains responsible to the *Purchaser* for Providing the Goods and Services, as defined by clause 11.2(13).

24.2 This clause provides that the *Supplier* may subcontract parts of his work provided the *Supply Manager* accepts the proposed Subcontractor.

Acceptance of a Subcontractor cannot be withdrawn later, provided his appointment complies with these clauses. Where national or international law requires, the Goods Information should include a statement of award criteria for subcontractors.

The *Supplier* cannot appoint a proposed Subcontractor until the *Supply Manager* has accepted him.

Other responsibilities 25

25.1 This clause requires the *Supplier* to obtain the requisite approvals of his design from, for example, railway inspectorates, nuclear inspectorates or relevant other organisations who may have the duty or authority to approve his design.

25.2 It is important that the *Supply Manager* has the right to visit places where work is being carried out or materials and plant stored in connection with the contract. This includes right of access to suppliers' and Subcontractors' premises to allow inspection and testing, and to check progress.

This right of visit and inspection can be extended to Others notified to the *Supplier* by the *Supply Manager*. The final part of the clause is designed to protect the *Supplier* from the *Supply Manager* notifying people who may have a connection with the *Supplier*'s competitors. The *Supplier* cannot restrict access which is required by the Goods Information or the applicable law.

25.3 Various clauses in the contract give the *Supply Manager* authority to issue instructions to the *Supplier*. These instructions should be given within the limits and for the reasons expressly stated. This clause requires the *Supplier* to obey such instructions.

If for any reason the *Supplier* disagrees with an instruction, having exhausted the procedures in the contract for dealing with such a situation, his remedy is to follow the disputes procedure in clause 94. He should not refuse to obey the instruction.

25.4 Any specific health and safety requirements relating to the *goods* and *services*, including the requirements as to the supply, should be stated in the Goods Information. These are additional to any obligations the *Supplier* may have under national law where the *goods* are being manufactured or the *law of the contract* or both.

25.5 This clause requires the *Supplier* to obtain the requisite approvals of his arrangements for the transport of the *goods* from relevant other organisations, such as customs and/or border officials, government inspectors, highway authorities or others who may have the duty or authority to approve his proposals and give permission.

3 Time

CORE CLAUSES

Starting and Delivery **30**

30.1 The *starting date* is decided by the *Purchaser* and stated in Contract Data part one. The *delivery date* is stated in the Contract Data by either the *Purchaser* or the *Supplier*, depending on the *Purchaser's* requirements. If the procurement process and appointment of the *Supplier* takes longer than anticipated, it may be necessary to adjust the *starting date* and *delivery date* by agreement before the Contract Date.

For many contracts the *delivery date* is decided by the *Purchaser*. Alternatively the *delivery date* may be decided by the tenderers and submitted as part of their offers. If this is done, the *Purchaser* should make clear how tenders are to be assessed, indicating the value to be placed on an early *delivery date.*

It is essential for the *delivery date* to be stated by one of the above methods. If this is not done various provisions of the contract cannot be applied (for example the payment provisions or delay damages).

For some contracts there may be more than one Delivery and therefore more than one Delivery Date. (See clause 12.5). For example the contract is for the provision of three sets of rolling stock and each set is for Delivery on a different date.

If this is the case each *delivery date* must be stated in the Contract Data using one of the above methods.

30.2 The *Purchaser* may require control over when the *goods* are brought to the delivery place by the *Supplier.* For example he may need to arrange the availability of specialist equipment to unload the *goods.* This clause allows the *Purchaser* to state in the Contract Data that the *Supplier* may not bring the *goods* to the delivery place more than one week before the Delivery Date and therefore the *Supplier* has to arrange his transport to comply with this requirement.

The programme **31**

31.1 Provision is made in the Contract Data for a *Supplier's* programme to be identified in the Contract Data part two or to be submitted by the *Supplier* after the Contract Date, but within the period stated in the Contract Data part one.

The *Supplier* is required to provide a programme to the *Supply Manager* for his acceptance. This programme should be updated at regular intervals by the *Supplier* and re-issued to the *Supply Manager* for his acceptance.

The programme is an important document for administering the contract. It informs the *Purchaser* and the *Supply Manager* of the *Supplier's* detailed intentions of how he is to Provide the Goods and Services. It enables the *Supply Manager* to monitor the *Supplier's* performance and to assess the effects of compensation events.

Purchaser's will normally elect to have the programme submitted with tenders in order to judge whether a tenderer has fully understood his obligations and whether he is able to supply the *goods* and *services* in the time periods proposed using the methods and resources proposed. Any doubts on these matters can then be discussed and resolved after submission of tenders. In accepting a tender which includes a *Supplier's* programme, it is important that the *Purchaser* makes clear that such acceptance does not warrant that the methods and resources are adequate.

31.2 This clause lists the information which the *Supplier* is required to show on each programme submitted for acceptance. In some cases this may be very comprehensive and the programme is likely to be a series of documents, not just a simple bar chart.

The following notes are broadly in the same order as the bullets in the clause.

- The programme dates will be those stated in the Contract Data or changed in accordance with the contract (see explanatory notes on clauses 11.2(6), 30, 36, 63.4 and 63.5). The Delivery Date can only be moved in the programme because of an implemented compensation event (clause 65.1) or an agreed acceleration (clause 35).
- The *Supplier* should plan Delivery for both the manufacturing and fabrication work required by the Goods Information (including design if required) and the supply of the *goods* required by the Supply Requirements. The programme is updated as the work progresses. It is important to understand that planned Delivery is not the same as the Delivery Date. The former is the date that the *Supplier* is forecasting that Delivery (clause 11.2(5)) will be achieved, and will be linked to the critical path of the programme; the latter is the date by which the contract requires the *Supplier* to have achieved Delivery (clause 30.1).
- The dates when the *Supplier* will need things provided by the *Purchaser* and Others, for example specific information or acceptances required by the contract, as well as access to the *Purchaser*'s premises.
- The dates when the *Supplier* plans to conduct tests and inspections.

Other information which the Goods Information requires is a broad obligation and could include such matters as

- The provision for health and safety matters specifically mentioned in the Goods Information. (The *Supplier* should also allow for any statutory procedures).
- The specific order and timing of the *Supplier*'s own work which may include activities for the manufacture and fabrication, prototyping, tests, inspections and transportation of the *goods* as well as any *services* activities that are required. This should be updated regularly to reflect the actual progress of the work. (See clause 32.1).
- The dates when the *Supplier* plans to complete work to an extent that will allow the *Purchaser* and Others to do their work. This work should be described in the Goods Information.
- The *Supplier*'s time risk allowances attached to the duration of each activity or to the duration of parts of the work. These allowances are owned by the *Supplier* as part of his realistic planning to cover his risks. They should be either clearly identified as such in the programme or included in the time periods allocated to specific activities. It follows that they should be retained in the assessment of any delay to planned Delivery due to the effect of a compensation event.
- The *Supplier*'s float allowance which is any spare time within the programme after the time risk allowances have been included. It is normally available to accommodate the time effects of a compensation event in order to mitigate or avoid any delay to planned Delivery. However, float attached to the whole programme (i.e. any float between planned Delivery and the Delivery Date) is not available to deal with compensation events. Any delay to planned Delivery due to a compensation event therefore results in the same delay to the Delivery Date.
- It is important that the time risk allowances and float included by the *Supplier* in a programme submitted for acceptance are realistic. If they are not, the *Supply Manager* may refer to the third bullet of clause 31.3 and refuse acceptance.
- The *Purchaser* should ensure that the Goods Information states the operations for which he requires detailed method statements, or other specific information shown in the programme.

31.3   When the *Supplier* issues a programme or revised programme for acceptance the *Supply Manager* must reply accepting or rejecting it within two weeks. Failure to do so by this time will be a compensation event – see clause 60.1(6).

This clause lists reasons why a *Supply Manager* may decide not to accept a programme or revised programme. Rejection by the *Supply Manager* of a programme for these reasons will not be a compensation event – see clause 13.8. Rejection for reasons other than those stated is a compensation event – see clause 60.1(8).

Acceptance of the *Supplier's* programme, unlike acceptance of the *Supplier's* design, is not a condition precedent to the *Supplier* proceeding with his work. Failure to accept a programme or revised programme does not require the *Supplier* to stop work.

If the *Supply Manager's* reply is non-acceptance, the *Supplier* is required to re-submit within the *period for reply*.

Revising the programme   **32**

32.1   This clause lists the matters which are to be shown on a revised programme. It should record the actual progress achieved on each operation and the reprogramming of future operations. It should allow for the effects of any future events that the *Supplier* is aware of, whether they are compensation events or not. This may change the date of planned Delivery. However the Delivery Date will not change unless a compensation event has been implemented or an acceleration has been agreed (see explanatory notes on the first two bullets of clause 31.2).

The revised programme should also show proposals for dealing with delays, Defects and any changes the *Supplier* wishes to make.

Failure by the *Supplier* to submit revised programmes is of considerable disadvantage to him in that if a compensation event occurs, the *Supply Manager* may assess it based upon his own assessment of what the programme should be. Thus it is in the *Supplier's* interests to keep the programme up to date and maintain the existence of an Accepted Programme.

32.2   The *Supply Manager* should note, in reviewing a submitted revised programme, any changes to the dates by which the *Purchaser* is required to provide information, facilities, possession, etc. He should be prepared to accept a programme with earlier dates if this is acceptable to the *Purchaser*. After acceptance, any subsequent failure by the *Purchaser* to meet these earlier dates would be a compensation event.

Access   **33**

33.1   The *Purchaser* is required to allow access to and use of his premises to the *Supplier* as necessary for his work. This could be access for Delivery of the *goods*, to undertake a *service*, or both.

Instructions to stop or not to start work   **34**

34.1   This clause gives the *Supply Manager* authority to control the stopping and re-starting of work being carried out by the *Supplier*, including work by the *Supplier's* Subcontractors or suppliers, for any reason. An instruction given under this clause constitutes a compensation event under clause 60.1(4), unless if it arises from a fault of the *Supplier*, in which case the Prices are not changed – see clause 61.4. In certain circumstances, if the *Supply Manager* fails to instruct the re-start of work within thirteen weeks of instructing work to stop, the *Supplier* may be entitled to terminate the performance of the contract. (See clause 91.6).

Acceleration   **35**

Acceleration under this contract means bringing the Delivery Date forward, i.e. requiring the *Supplier* to make the supply sooner than he is contractually obliged to. This therefore differs from the usage in many other contracts where 'acceleration' means speeding up the supply to ensure that Delivery is achieved by the Delivery Date, i.e. trying to make sure that the *Supplier* achieves what he is contractually obliged to do.

If this latter case applies the *Supply Manger* should not instruct a quotation for acceleration, as that would effectively mean paying the *Supplier* extra in order to achieve what he is obliged to achieve anyway. If the *Supply Manager* is concerned that delay which has already occurred, and which is not as a result of a compensation event, may result in the Delivery Date not being achieved, he should instead instruct the *Supplier* to produce a revised programme (see clause 32.2) to show how he intends to recover the time he has lost.

35.1
35.2 These clauses allow the *Supply Manager* (normally at the request of the *Purchaser*) to instruct a quotation for acceleration from the *Supplier*. There is no remedy if it is not produced or if the *Supplier's* quotation is unacceptable. Acceleration cannot be imposed on the *Supplier* without his agreement.

4 Testing and Defects

CORE CLAUSES

Supplier's quality obligations	The *Supplier's* responsibility for quality is part of his duty to Provide the Goods and Services (clause 20.1) as defined in clause 11.2(13).

The quality standards to be achieved by the *Supplier* for the *goods* and *services* should be specified in the Goods Information. These standards provide the basis on which the existence of a Defect is judged (clause 11.2(3)). The *Supply Manager* acts on the *Purchaser's* behalf to check the *Supplier's* attainment of the specified standards suppliers generally manufacture and fabricate to national standards.

Quality systems

High value goods of the type likely to be supplied under this contract will most likely be described in detail in the *Purchaser's* Goods Information, but more in the form of a performance specification. In many cases the *goods* may not be easily compared or matched against other *goods* of a similar nature. For instance a gas turbine of one supplier cannot readily be compared against a gas turbine of another supplier. Products from different manufacturers are not always easily interchangeable.

If quality systems are required, they should be initiated by the *Purchaser* at an early stage, such as at the early design stages if the *goods* are bespoke to the *Purchaser*. The *Purchaser* may specify his requirements for the quality management system in the Goods Information.

Warranties and guarantees

Most suppliers will be familiar with the terms warranty and guaranty. However to avoid potential conflict with the meaning given to these terms in different jurisdictions, the NEC approach is to require the *Supplier* to correct Defects whether notified or not until the *defects date*. The Contract Data identifies the *defects date* as a period of time in weeks after Delivery. If that period is identified as 52 weeks, this will equate to a "warranty" of 12 months. If there are multiple Delivery Dates for the *goods* each Delivery will have its own *defects date* (or 'warranty'). As a Defect is a part of the *goods* and *services* which is not in accordance with the Goods Information (see clause 11.2(3)) the extent of the 'warranty' depends on the Goods Information.

Tests and inspections **40**

Clause 40 does not apply to tests and inspections done by the *Supplier* at his own discretion and for his own purposes. It only applies to tests and inspections which the *Purchaser* has specified in the Goods Information or those required by the applicable law.

40.1

Tests which the *Purchaser* is likely to specify could include factory acceptance tests before preparation for the transport of the *goods* and tests after Delivery as part of the *services*.

The applicable law from the *Purchaser's* point of view is likely to be that applicable in the location where the *goods* are to be used. Although the *goods* may have been manufactured to international standards such as BS or DIN, there may be some additional or alternative constraints in the country where they are to be used, such as emissions or exposure to harsh climatic conditions.

40.2

Whilst the *Supplier* is likely to be doing most of the testing with the *Supply Manager* as a witness, certainly before Delivery, this clause caters for things which the *Purchaser* may need to provide. The information relating to records, data sheets, materials, facilities and samples for tests and inspections specified in Goods Information is likely to be compiled jointly by the Parties based on *Supplier*'s manufacturing methods and timing as well as the *Purchaser*'s requirements on how the *goods* are to be put to use.

The tests should be specified in the Goods Information with respect to

- the nature of the tests,
- the stage in the manufacturing process when they are to be done,
- their objectives and
- whether or not payment or authorisation to proceed to the next stage of the supply depends on the test results.

Additional tests may be instructed by the *Supply Manager* by changing the Goods Information. This is a compensation event under clause 60.1(1) unless the test is either required to check for a Defect and one is found (clause 60.1(9)) or it is a repeat test. Such instructions should specify details of the test.

| When tests are to be done | Significant stages may include the following. |

- Prototype testing.
- Factory Acceptance Tests of manufactured *goods*.
- Before payment for or marking of *goods* (clause 71.1).
- Before Delivery (clause 41.1). The Goods Information should state which tests have to be passed before Delivery.
- After Delivery but before the *defects date*. The *Purchaser* may require some tests to be done of the *goods* in use, for example where the *goods* are a train set for a new fast commuter network. Such tests may be carried out by the *Supply Manager* on the *Purchaser*'s behalf but most likely by the *Supplier* as part of the *services*.

Failure by the *Supply Manager* to carry out his tests promptly is a compensation event (clause 60.1(10)) if it causes unnecessary delay to the *Supplier*.

| Where tests are to be done | The Goods Information should state the location of each test. This may include the premises of one of the *Supplier*'s Subcontractors, the *Supplier*'s own premises and the location where the *goods* are to be used. |

| Who does the test | The Goods Information should specify who is responsible for carrying out each test or for arranging for it to be carried out. The choice will be between the following. |

- The *Supplier*, including his Subcontractors and suppliers. Where the *Supplier* is to arrange for a test to be carried out by an independent or public authority, the Goods Information should include the name of the authority, the tests and the form in which the results are to be supplied.
- The *Supply Manager*.

| Who provides materials, facilities and samples | The Goods Information should state who provides the materials and apparatus necessary for each test. The required items may include the following. |

- Samples of materials to be tested. These are normally provided by the *Supplier*, his Subcontractors or suppliers.
- Testing apparatus, test loads, measuring instruments. These could be provided by the *Purchaser* or the *Supplier* (including his Subcontractors or suppliers) or hired from an independent or public authority.
- Testing facilities (normally provided by the *Supplier* but sometimes by the *Purchaser*) or laboratories of an independent company or authority.

| Objectives, procedures, etc. | The objectives, procedures and the standards to be satisfied should be specified in the Goods Information. Types of tests may include the following. |

- Testing the properties of materials to be incorporated in the *goods* for strength, durability, appearance, brittleness, flexibility, corrosion resistance, etc.

- Testing the performance, accuracy and reliability of control systems and associated instruments and servo-mechanisms incorporated in the *goods*.
- Testing the reliability, safety and effectiveness of electrical, mechanical and other systems incorporated in the *goods*.
- Testing the performance of the goods to prove that they perform as specified in the Goods Information.

40.3 This clause deals with four matters

- the procedure for notifying when testing is to be done,
- the requirement to notify test results,
- the timing of notifying the *Supply Manager* of testing or inspection, and
- the right of the *Supply Manager* to observe the *Supplier* tests.

The *Supplier* and *Supply Manager* are each required to give the other advance notice of tests which each is to carry out. This enables both Parties to be fully informed and to take any action they wish to take. If, for example, testing reveals that some work does not comply with the Goods Information, early discussion of the consequences is likely to be required. Notification of tests and their results is required before further testing or inspection is rendered impossible or impracticable. Failure by the *Supplier* to notify the *Supply Manager* of a test or inspection may deprive the *Supplier* of compensation for a search, even if no Defect is found (clause 60.1(9)).

40.4 A Defect is defined in clause 11.2(3). Any repeat test or inspection of work after a Defect has been corrected is not a compensation event.

A Defect may make it impossible to refabricate the *goods* affected in accordance with the Goods Information. The early warning procedure (clause 16) requires early discussion of the matter. Possible solutions include changing the Goods Information after redesign or accepting the Defect (clause 44).

If Option X17 is used low performance damages may be due if a Defect is still uncorrected by a *defects date*.

40.5 Under this clause, the *Supply Manager* is required to carry out testing and inspection for which he is responsible so that unnecessary delay to the supply is avoided. Some payments to the *Supplier* may be conditional upon doing particular tests (for example factory acceptance tests) to show that the work has been carried out satisfactorily. If the *Supply Manager* causes unnecessary delay it is a compensation event results (clause 60.1(10)).

40.6 If a test has to be repeated following the discovery of a Defect, the *Supplier* pays the *Supply Manager*'s assessment of the cost incurred by the *Purchaser*. Such costs could include charges and expenses invoiced to the *Purchaser* by an independent testing agency he used to witness tests or inspection on his behalf as a result of having to witness the tests twice or come back on a separate occasion to do so.

Performance testing of the *goods*

To prove that *goods* meet reliability, performance and other parameters, it is often necessary to test them before transport to the delivery place or even before a full manufacturing programme is undertaken.

The SC test and inspection provisions allow for any combination of tests to be carried out before and after Delivery. There is therefore no need to have separate clauses in the *conditions of contract* (or include additional conditions using Option Z) to deal with different types of test.

Many combinations of tests may be required for the *goods* and it is not practical for the *conditions of contract* to prescribe particular tests. The *Purchaser* must state in the Goods Information what tests are required (see notes on clause 40.2), in a similar way to drafting a detailed traditional specification.

It may be useful to include in the Goods Information a schedule tabulating details of the tests to be done at different stages of the supply and post Delivery with cross-references to the relevant sections of the Goods Information containing the detailed procedures.

Testing and inspection before Delivery 41

41.1 The purpose of this clause is to avoid expense in having to transport *goods* back to the place of manufacture if testing and inspection reveal Defects. Users should note this is only referring to tests and inspection which the Goods Information requires. Most suppliers will have their own test regime in any case.

In order to avoid conflict the Goods Information should state clearly what the test or inspection comprises, and at what point or in accordance with what criteria the test or inspection of the *goods* has passed.

Searching for and notifying Defects 42

42.1 The *Supplier* is responsible for correcting a Defect as defined in clause 11.2(3). A fault in a design provided by the *Purchaser* is not a Defect.

If a search is instructed and a defect is found which is due to a fault in the *Purchaser's* design (i.e. no Defect as defined is found), the instruction to search is a compensation event (clause 60.1(9)) and responsibility for further action belongs to the *Supply Manager*. He may decide to change the design and instruct the *Supplier* accordingly. This would constitute a change to the Goods Information, which would be a further compensation event (clause 60.1(1)).

If the defect is due to non-compliance with the Goods Information, it is a Defect and does not result in a compensation event. It is then the *Supplier's* responsibility to correct the Defect so that the *goods* and *services* comply with the Goods Information.

The clause also includes extra tests and inspections not specified in the Goods Information within the meaning of 'searching'. Whether or not such tests are compensation events is determined using clause 60.1(10).

42.2 The intention of this clause is to enable Defects to be identified as soon as possible so that they can be dealt with promptly.

The periods for the notification and correction of Defects are illustrated in Figure 1.

The *defects date* is defined in the Contract Data as a date which is a stated period of time after Delivery. Normal practice would be to equate this period to the warranty or guarantee period typically made available by a supplier for the type of goods being procured. This could be anything from 12 months to 36 months.

Defects may be notified for correction by the *Supplier* at any time before the *defects date*. The *defects date* is the earliest date when the *Supplier* ceases to be liable under the contract for the correction of Defects. However, the *Supplier's* liability to correct Defects under the contract after Delivery may continue after the *defects date* for the *defect correction period* if a Defect is notified just before the *defects date* (see Figure 1).

The *Supply Manager* or *Purchaser* may inform the *Supplier* of Defects after the *defects date* but the *Supplier's* responsibility for them may be limited according to the law governing the contract or by the operation of clause 88.

Correcting Defects 43

43.1 The *Supplier* is responsible for correcting all Defects, whether notified or not.

Before Delivery, the *Supplier* is responsible for correcting all Defects which would prevent him fulfilling his obligation to Provide the Goods and Services in accordance with the Goods Information (clause 20.1). He therefore needs to

correct Defects in time to avoid delaying Delivery, as defined in clause 11.2(5).

Figure 1. Notification and correction of Defects.

1. Defects found by *Supplier* (S) or notified by *Supply Manager* (SM) before Delivery:

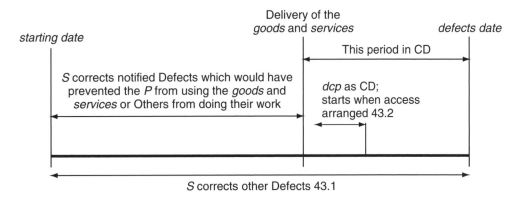

2. Defects notified by *Supply Manager* (SM) after Delivery and before *defects date*:

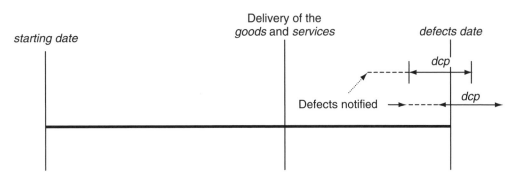

If Defects not corrected within *dcp*, SM assesses cost of correction by other people and paid by S (45.1).

3. Defects found after *defects date*:

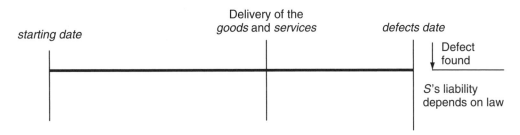

Key: *SM* = *Supply Manager*; *S* = *Supplier*; *CD* = *Contract Data*; *P* = *Purchaser*; *dcp* = *defect correction period*.

43.2   After Delivery, the *Supplier* is required to correct any remaining notified Defects, which would not have delayed Delivery, before the end of the *defect correction period*. The *defect correction period*, stated in part one of the Contract Data, only affect the timing of correcting Defects after Delivery. Provision is made in the Contract Data format for different lengths of *defect correction period* which may be appropriate for different types of Defect. The length of the *defect correction period* for each type of Defect to be given in the Contract Data depends on

- the kind of Defects likely to be outstanding after Delivery and the time needed for their correction,

- the urgency of the *Purchaser*'s need for their correction,
- the practicality of the *Supplier* being able to provide replacement *goods* or
- have the necessary people available to correct the *goods* in the location where they are being used.

An example of a high degree of urgency for a Defect to be corrected would be one found after Delivery which prevents the *Purchaser* from using the *goods*. The *defect correction period* for such a Defect should be stated in the Contract Data part should be short. If the *Supplier* is then unable to comply, the *Purchaser* is allowed to have the Defect corrected by other people and recover the incurred cost from the *Supplier* (see explanatory notes on clause 45.1).

The *defect correction period* starts when the access necessary for the *Supplier* to correct the Defect has been arranged by the *Supply Manager*. This is because the *goods* containing the Defect may have subsequently been installed as part of an operating facility, which may not be owned or operated by the *Purchaser*.

43.3 Further damage to the *goods* or *services* could arise if for whatever reason the *Supplier* is not given access necessary to correct a Defect as soon as possible. The *Supplier* is not held liable for damage to the *goods* or *services* that occur later than the end of the *defect access period* after notification. The combination of this clause and clause 43.2 motivates the *Purchaser* and the *Supply Manager* to arrange for the necessary access to be given before the end of the *defect access period* following notification. If this is not done and damage then occurs as a result of the Defect, the *Supplier* is not liable for this later damage (but remains liable for any damage that occurred before the end of the *defect access period*).

The *defect access periods* should take into account how different types of Defects might affect operation. For complex plant the Goods Information should include a procedure for dealing with commissioning and the initial operating regime, taking into account the *defect access periods* and including the criteria that the *Supply Manager* will apply in deciding if the Defect does require an immediate notification to the *Supplier* (possibly leading to a shutdown of the affected plant), or if the plant can be safely allowed to operate before giving access to the *Supplier*.

Accepting Defects 44

44.1 Although a Defect may be minor, its correction may be costly to the *Supplier* and may delay Delivery by a considerable time. Its correction may also cause inconvenience to the *Purchaser* out of all proportion to the benefits gained. This clause gives a procedure within the contract for accepting a Defect in these circumstances. Either the *Supplier* or the *Supply Manager* may propose a change to the Goods Information solely to avoid the need to correct a Defect. The other is not obliged to accept the proposal.

44.2 The *Supplier*'s quotation for the proposed change will show a reduction in either time or price or both. In some cases the reduction may be nominal. For example, a nominal price reduction may be acceptable if the effect of the change to the Goods Information is not detrimental and if the alternative of correcting the Defect will reduce the likelihood of prompt Delivery.

If the quotation is not acceptable, no further action is necessary. If the quotation is accepted by the *Supply Manager*, the Goods Information, the Prices and the Delivery Date are changed accordingly. Such a change to the Goods Information is not a compensation event (clause 60.1(1)).

If the Defect is notified after the Delivery Date, there cannot be any change to the Delivery Date, but a reduced Price may apply.

In terms of liability, the consequences are the same as for other changes to the Goods Information. In other words, when the *Supply Manager* accepts a Defect and the reduced Prices and earlier Delivery Date are agreed, the *Supplier* cannot continue to be held liable for the specific Defect, as if the Defect had still to be corrected under clause 43.1.

Uncorrected Defects 45

45.1   This clause states the procedure if the *Supplier* fails to correct a Defect having been given the necessary access. Correction by other people (as distinct from ''by Others'') could allow the *Purchaser* to have the Defect corrected by the *Supplier*'s Subcontractors.

The *Supply Manager*'s assessment of the cost of correcting the Defect would need to be deducted from any amounts still owing to the *Supplier* or invoiced to him as an amount due. There is no provision for retention to be held in the SC.

45.2   This clause states the procedure if the Defect has not been corrected due to the lack of access. The criteria the *Supply Manager* uses to assess the amount to be paid is an assessment of the *Supplier*'s cost for carrying out the correction. This may be lower than that assessed in clause 45.1. It will rarely, if ever, be higher, given that the *Supplier* could also employ other people to correct the Defect.

5 Payment

CORE CLAUSES

Assessing the amount due **50**

50.1 This clause determines 'assessment dates' from which the dates of both certification and payment are calculated. The first assessment date is determined by the *Supply Manager*, preferably after discussion with the *Supplier*, with a view to satisfying the internal procedures of both the *Purchaser* and the *Supplier*. Thereafter, assessment dates occur after each *assessment interval* until four weeks after the last *defects date*.

50.2 The payment mechanism is based on the use of the Price Schedule and the Prices. The Price Schedule included in the contract provides the pricing information needed for assessing the amount due. Notes on the Price Schedule are included in Chapter 3 of these Guidance Notes.

The Prices are defined in clause 11.2(11). The second sentence of the definition provides for the pricing of those items for which a quantity and rate are stated in the Price Schedule.

Payments for an item do not become due until the item described has been completed unless a quantity and a rate are stated in the Price Schedule for the item, in which case only the Price for the quantity completed is included. It is important that the item descriptions are carefully written with appropriate references to the Goods Information, including testing requirements.

All other payments, except advanced payments, such as VAT and sales tax, and payments by the *Supplier* for failure to correct Defects, are added or deducted to calculate the amount due.

Under the United Kingdom's VAT regulations, payment of VAT by the *Purchaser* to the *Supplier* is made in response to a VAT invoice provided by the *Supplier*. The *Supply Manager* and the *Supplier* should therefore make arrangements to ensure that

- the correct levels of VAT are included in the amount due and
- the *Supplier*'s VAT invoice is provided for attachment to the *Supply Manager*'s payment certificate.

It is recommended that the Parties should agree, at the start of the contract, how the administration of sales tax documentation should be dealt with as part of the payment procedure.

50.3 Although assessments of the amount due are the responsibility of the *Supply Manager*, he takes account of any submissions by the *Supplier* and provides details to the *Supplier* of his assessment.

Payment **51**

51.1 The latest dates by which the *Supply Manager* certifies payments are fixed throughout a contract as each is related to an assessment date. In the majority of cases, certification will be of payment to the *Supplier*.

51.2 The latest dates by which payments are due to be made are also fixed throughout a contract as each is related to an assessment date. Interest is due to the receiving Party, either *Purchaser* or *Supplier*, if a payment is not made within the stated period after the assessment date. The *Supply Manager* should

- certify payment as early as possible within the week after the assessment date and

- before the Contract Date, check that the *Purchaser* is able to pay within the stated period after the assessment date.

The principle that interest is due from the latest date that payment should have been made is applied throughout the contract.

51.3 The same principles on interest due apply to later corrections to certified amounts (including any due to compensation events) made by the *Supply Manager* or decided by the *Adjudicator* or the *tribunal*. The last sentence of this clause refers to interest being calculated from the date upon which the increased amount would have been certified if there had been no dispute or mistake.

51.4 The *interest rate* stated in part one of the Contract Data should be a reliable annual base rate applicable to the territory in which the work is to be done plus a percentage to represent the current commercial rates. This may be, for example, 2% above the base rate. Simple interest at the *interest rate* applies for periods less than one year.

Defined Cost 52

52.1 Defined Cost is defined in clause 11.2(4). The only use of Defined Cost is as the basis of the assessment of compensation events. (See the notes on clause 63). Defined Cost is the cost of the components listed in the definition that make up the amount paid by the *Supplier* in Providing the Goods and Services whether he subcontracts work or not. The cost of preparing quotations for compensation events is specifically excluded.

This clause sets the boundary on the *Supplier*'s costs which are not included in Defined Cost as being those costs he includes for his overheads in the *percentage for overheads and profit*. The *Supplier*'s profit is also included in the percentage.

The Price Schedule 53

53.1 This clause emphasises the fact that the Price Schedule is only a payment document. It cannot be used to determine what work, *goods* and *services* the *Supplier* is to provide only to determine payments to the *Supplier* for what he provides.

6 Compensation events

CORE CLAUSES

Compensation events	**60**	Compensation events are events which, if they occur and do not arise from the *Supplier*'s fault, entitle the *Supplier* to be compensated for any effect the event may have on the Prices or the Delivery Date. A compensation event will normally result in additional payment to the *Supplier* but in a few cases may result in reduced payment.

Compensation events are listed in these core clauses. The main list is in clause 60.1; this includes events (1) to (15). Further compensation events are stated in Options X2.1, X12.3(6), X12.3(7) and X14.2.

Option Z may be used by the *Purchaser* to insert additional compensation events. The effect of such additions is to transfer the financial risk of the events from the *Supplier* to the *Purchaser*. The event must be described precisely.

Changing the Goods Information   **60.1 (1)**

Changes to the *goods* and *services* are made by a *Supply Manager*'s instruction to change the Goods Information. The authority given to the *Supply Manager* for this purpose is in clause 14.3. Changes may comprise deletions from, or additions to, the Goods Information. There may be many reasons for changing the Goods Information. For example a change to the *Purchaser*'s technical requirements, a change made to eliminate an illegality or impossibility (clause 18.1) or to resolve an ambiguity or inconsistency (clause 17.1).

This clause states two exceptions to a change to the Goods Information being a compensation event.

- The procedure for accepting a Defect is stated in clause 44. An instruction to change the Goods Information after acceptance of the *Supplier*'s quotation under clause 44.1 is not a compensation event.
- A change to the *Supplier*'s design made at his own request is not a compensation event. This clause also gives precedence to the Goods Information provided by the *Purchaser* over the Goods Information provided by the *Supplier*. Thus the *Supplier* should ensure that the Goods Information he prepares and submits with his tender complies with the requirements of the Goods Information provided by the *Purchaser*. (See also notes on clause 21.2.)

Access (2)

The *Purchaser*'s obligation to provide access to and use of his premises and when is stated in clause 33.1. The *Supplier* is required to include this information in his programme under clause 31.2.

Provision by the *Purchaser* (3)

The Goods Information should give details of anything which the *Purchaser* is to provide, such as equipment, plant and materials, and of any restrictions on when it is to be provided. The *Supplier* is required to include this information in his programme under clause 31.2.

Stopping work (4)

Clause 34.1 gives the *Supply Manager* authority to instruct the *Supplier* to stop or not to start work. There are several reasons why the *Supply Manager* may wish to give such an instruction, for example, for reasons of safety or because of operational risks.

Work of the *Purchaser* (5)

The Goods Information should give details of the order and timing of work to be done by the *Purchaser* and people acting on his behalf. The *Supplier* is required to include this in the information in his programme under clause 31.2.

Reply to a communication	(6)	Various periods are given in particular clauses for reply by the *Supply Manager* and a general (or in some cases specific) *period for reply* is given in the Contract Data. The obligation to reply within the relevant period is stated in clause 13.3.
Changing a decision	(7)	The *Supply Manager* is able to change a decision made under the authority given to him in the contract, in the same way that he made the original decision.
Withholding acceptance	(8)	Various clauses state reasons why the *Supply Manager* is entitled not to accept a submission or proposal from the *Supplier*. Rejection of a submission or proposal for reasons other than those stated is a compensation event.
Searching	(9)	The *Supply Manager* can instruct the *Supplier* to search for a Defect under clause 42.1. Usually searches are instigated where faulty design or manufacture is suspected.
Delayed tests or inspections	(10)	Testing and inspection work to be carried out by the *Supply Manager* is stated in the Goods Information. Under clause 40.5, the *Supply Manager* is required to do this without causing unnecessary delay. Wherever possible, the Goods Information should include practical estimates of the time the *Supply Manager* needs for any of his tests. This will avoid arguments about what constitutes "unnecessary" delay.
Records, data sheets, materials, facilities and samples for tests and inspections	(11)	Under clause 40.2 the *Purchaser* is required to provide records, data sheets, materials, facilities and samples for tests and inspections as stated in the Goods Information.
Purchaser's risks	(12)	*Purchaser*'s risks are stated in clause 80.1. Any additional *Purchaser*'s risks should be stated in part one of the Contract Data.
Assumptions about compensation events	(13)	Under clause 61.6, the *Supply Manager* may state assumptions to be used in assessing compensation events. If he later notifies corrections to these assumptions, the notification is a separate compensation event under this clause.
		These assumptions should not be confused with any forecast or estimate made by the *Supplier* in his assessment of a compensation event. If the *Supplier*'s forecast is later shown to have been wrong, neither the *Supplier* nor *Supply Manager* can change it. (See clause 65.2).
Purchaser's breach of contract	(14)	This is an 'umbrella' clause to include breaches of contract by the *Purchaser* within the compensation event procedure. Without this clause, in most jurisdictions the *Supplier*'s only remedy for a breach of contract by the *Purchaser* would be under the law. However, because of the effects of this clause and clause 63.4, the *Supplier*'s only remedy is under the contract.
Prevention event	(15)	This is a "force majeure" event; however it is limited to an event during the transport of the *goods* to the Delivery Place. The event must be such that it either stops Delivery by the *Supplier* (an absolute test) or stops Delivery by the *Supplier* by the Delivery Date. (See the notes on clause 19.1).
Notifying compensation events	**61**	
	61.1	This procedure would normally apply to compensation events 1, 4, 7, 9 and 13 each of which is due to an action by the *Supply Manager*. When the event occurs, the *Supply Manager* notifies the *Supplier* and instructs him to submit quotations. Where the compensation event results from the *Supplier*'s fault or where quotations have already been submitted, quotations are not instructed. However, in order to avoid doubt in such cases, it is advisable that when the *Supply Manager* notifies the compensation event, he should give his reason for not instructing quotations. The *Supplier* is required to act on the instruction or changed decision.
		It is important that the *Supply Manager* notifies such compensation events, without waiting for the *Supplier* to do so. If he does not do so he may leave the *Purchaser* open to late claims from the *Supplier*, because the time-bar in clause 61.3 does not apply to these types of event.

61.2   This clause deals with the situation where the *Supply Manager* is considering issuing an instruction or changing a decision but first requires to know what effect this would have on cost and time, for example, when he is considering a change to the Goods Information (clause 60.1(1)). He has authority to instruct the *Supplier* to submit quotations as a first step.

61.3   This procedure would normally apply to the compensation events not covered by those in clause 61.1. These are events which arise from

- a failure by the *Purchaser* or *Supply Manager* to fulfil their obligations (compensation events 2, 3, 5, 6, 9, 10, 11 and 14),
- the *Supply Manager* withholding an acceptance for a reason not stated in the contract (compensation event 8) or
- a happening not caused by any Party (compensation event 12 and 15).

It would also apply to an event which the *Supply Manager* has not notified under clause 61.1. In such cases, the *Supplier* initiates the procedure by notifying the *Supply Manager*.

To avoid having to deal with a compensation event long after it has occurred there is a time limit on notification by the *Supplier*. Failure to comply with the time limit "time-bars" the *Supplier* from any compensation for the event unless the event should have been notified by the *Supply Manager* under clause 61.1.

61.4   This clause deals with the *Supply Manager*'s response to the *Supplier*'s notification of compensation events under clause 61.3. It lists the four tests which the *Supply Manager* applies to an event notified by the *Supplier* in order to decide whether or not to instruct the *Supplier* to submit quotations for its effect. If the *Supply Manager* decides that the event does not pass any one of the tests, he notifies the *Supplier* and no further action is required unless the *Supplier* disputes the decision and refers it to the *Adjudicator* under the dispute resolution procedure.

In many circumstances, the *Supply Manager* will be able to give his decision within a week of the *Supplier*'s notification. With more complicated events, a longer period will be desirable to ensure adequate time for a properly considered decision. Provision is made for such longer periods subject to the *Supplier*'s agreement.

The final paragraph of this clause protects the *Supplier* against a delay by the *Supply Manager* in responding to the *Supplier*'s notification.

61.5   The *Supply Manager* should include, in an instruction to submit quotations, his decision on whether or not the *Supplier* gave an early warning which an experienced supplier could have given. This is necessary to permit the application of the sanction in clause 63.6.

61.6   In some cases, the nature of a compensation event may be such that it is impossible to prepare a sufficiently accurate quotation, e.g. where the quantum of work involved cannot be decided until the work is started. In these cases, quotations are submitted on the basis of assumptions stated by the *Supply Manager* in his instruction to the *Supplier*. If the assumptions later prove to be wrong, the *Supply Manager*'s notification of their correction is a separate compensation event – clause 60.1(13).

Apart from this situation, the assessment of a compensation event cannot later be revised – clause 65.2. The reason for this strict procedure is to motivate the Parties to decide the effects of a compensation event either before or soon after it occurs. Since each quotation includes due allowance for risk (clause 63.6), and the fact that the early warning procedure should minimise the effects of unexpected problems, the need for later review is minimal.

Quotations for
compensation events **62**

62.1 There may be several ways of adjusting plans for the supply to deal with a compensation event and its consequences. The procedure in this clause enables the *Supply Manager* to consider different options. For instance, it may be more beneficial to the *Purchaser* to achieve earlier Delivery at greater cost than an alternative later Delivery at a lower cost or have an additional *service* carried out quickly or at a more convenient time, but at a greater cost than might otherwise be the case. This clause also provides for the *Supplier* to submit quotations using methods other than those assumed in the *Supply Manager*'s instruction. For instance, the *Supplier* may be able to use a specialised item of equipment or a different manufacturing process, the availability of which the *Supply Manager* was unaware.

62.2 Quotations comprise a 'package' of time and money as, in most situations, it is impossible to consider either in isolation. The use of the term 'quotations' is not the same as the normal use in commerce, i.e. the free submission of an offer. Quotations are based on an assessment of forecast or recorded Defined Cost (clause 63.2) and time (clause 63.4) arising from the compensation event. As an alternative, if the *Supply Manager* and the *Supplier* both agree, the rates in the Price Schedule may be used to assess the change to the Prices, if the compensation event only changes quantities (clause 63.1). A build-up of each quotation is required to be submitted by the *Supplier*. If re-programming of remaining work is affected, the quotation should include a revised programme, showing, amongst other things any change to planned Delivery or a Delivery Date.

62.3 The time limits are intended to promote efficient management of the contract procedures. The four categories of reply by the *Supply Manager* are listed. The third category may result from the *Supply Manager* deciding not to proceed with a proposed change to the Goods Information. This may happen when the cost of the change is too high or interference with the *Purchaser*'s activities is too great. The *Supply Manager* has absolute discretion on whether to proceed.

62.4 This procedure permits revision of quotations within stated time limits. In practice, this will usually follow discussion between the *Supply Manager* and the *Supplier* on the details of the submitted quotations. When instructing a revised quotation the *Supply Manager* may alter or add to the assumptions made under clause 61.6.

62.5 This clause provides for the extension of the time limits for submitting and replying to quotations. It would be used for the more major or far reaching events. The *Supply Manager* and the *Supplier* must agree to the extension before the expiry of the times stated.

62.6 It is important that the *Supply Manager* does not delay responding to a quotation within the time allowed. The procedure in this clause is designed to deal with a situation where the *Supply Manager* does not reply within the time stated in the contract or a longer agreed time and continues not to do so having been reminded by the *Supplier*. Once the quotation is treated as accepted it is implemented (clause 65.1).

Assessing compensation **63**
events

63.1 This clause allows the *Supply Manager* and the *Supplier* to agree to the use of the rates and prices in the Price Schedule in the assessment of compensation events that only affect the quantities of work activity, *goods* and *services* to be done. This is most likely to be appropriate for small quantity changes and for simplicity, the rates in the Price Schedule are used to price the changed quantities.

63.2 Compensation events which cannot be assessed under clause 63.1 are assessed on the basis of their effect on Defined Cost plus the *percentage for overheads and profit*.

The Parties should, at an early stage in the contract, discuss and agree how each of the components of cost in Defined Cost are built up and where appropriate agree an understanding on the sources of these costs. For example, the build up of the costs for the people directly employed by the *Supplier* in his factory is likely to include wages and amounts the *Supplier* has to pay in the employment of his people.

Ideally, the assessment will be the forecast of Defined Cost of the work in providing the *goods* and *services* which is yet to be done, but it may include an element of incurred Defined Cost for work in providing the *goods* and *services* which has been done.

Where the work to be done is changed, it is important that the assessment is based upon the change in forecast or recorded Defined Cost. This clause gives no authority for the price for the originally specified work to be deleted and for the forecast Defined Cost plus the *percentage for overheads and profit* of all work now required to be used for the basis of the new price.

If the Goods Information originally included an item (a) which is now to be replaced by an item (b), the compensation event is assessed as the difference between the forecast Defined Cost for (a) and the forecast Defined Cost for (b), to which is added the *percentage for overheads and profit*. The original price for (a) does not enter the assessment, and instead the assessment (plus or minus) is applied to that original price. Similarly if the effect of the compensation event is to delete an item, the original price is not merely deleted. Instead the assessment is based upon the forecast Defined Cost plus *percentage for overheads and profit* of that item, which is then applied to the original price to end up with a positive or negative figure.

Clause 63.2 pinpoints the date when there is a switch from recorded Defined Cost to forecast Defined Cost included in a quotation. This ensures that whoever is making the assessment of the compensation event, that assessment is based upon the same principles. Therefore neither the *Supplier* nor *Supply Manager* can choose the switch date in order to suit their own purposes. Similarly the *Adjudicator* is also required to use this switch date when assessing compensation events.

For compensation events which the *Supply Manager* should notify under clause 61.1, the switch date will be the date of the communication which led to the compensation event, not the date when the compensation event was notified by either the *Supplier* or *Supply Manager*. For all other compensation events the switch date will be the date when the compensation event is notified.

These rules also apply to the situation where there is an instruction to submit a revised quotation under clauses 62.3 and 62.4. In that case the revised quotation will use the same switch date as the original quotation.

63.3   Only certain compensation events can reduce the Prices. (See the notes on clause 63.10).

63.4   No compensation event can result in a reduction in the time for supplying the *goods* and *services*. Only an acceleration as agreed under clause 35 or an accepted quotation for not correcting a Defect under clause 44.2 can result in an earlier Delivery Date.

The first stage in assessing whether the Delivery Date should be delayed as a result of a compensation event is to adjust the Accepted Programme to take account of the compensation event with any appropriate adjustments to time risk allowances (clause 63.7). Any float in the programme before planned Delivery is available to mitigate or avoid any consequential delay to planned Delivery. However, any terminal float between planned Delivery and the Delivery Date is not available. If planned Delivery is delayed, the Delivery Date is delayed by the same period. If planned Delivery is not delayed, the Delivery Date is unchanged.

63.5   This clause restricts the rights of the Parties in assessing the effects of a compensation event. If any of the compensation events occurs the Parties sole remedy is to use the compensation event procedure. Therefore if the *Purchaser* breaches the contract (60.1(14)), the *Supplier* must pursue this route rather than pursuing damages. This prevents the *Supplier* from trying to circumvent the time limits in the contract.

63.6 The *Supplier*'s duty to give an early warning is stated in clause 16.1. This clause states the sanction to be applied if the *Supplier* fails to give early warning. It is possible that early warning could have allowed action to be taken which would have reduced costs and caused less interference with the *Purchaser*'s activities. It is important that the *Supply Manager* notifies the *Supplier* of his decision that early warning should have been given (clause 61.5) so that the *Supplier* knows the correct basis for his assessment.

63.7 Allowances for risk must be included in forecasts of Defined Cost and Delivery in the same way that the *Supplier* allows for risks when pricing his tender. The value of the allowance is greater when the work involved is uncertain and there is a high chance of a *Supplier*'s risk happening. It is least when the uncertainties are small and when the work involved is to be done by whose output rates can be predicted relatively accurately.

If there is considerable uncertainty over the effects of a compensation event then the *Supply Manager* can decide, in consultation with the *Supplier* where appropriate, to limit the uncertainty by stating the assumptions the *Supplier* is to base his quotation on. In effect he is limiting the *Supplier*'s risk but not necessarily removing it. Risk allowances for cost and time are still permitted in the assessment.

63.8 This clause protects the *Purchaser* against inefficiency on the part of the *Supplier*.

63.9 This clause expresses the 'contra proferentem' rule, which interprets a clause containing an ambiguity or inconsistency against the party responsible for drafting the document in which it occurs.

63.10 Only the events stated in this clause can lead to the Prices being reduced. In addition, the Prices can be reduced by the application of Option X2.

63.12 It is not always practicable to use Defined Cost to assess Subcontractor's costs. This clause permits a sensible alternative method of assessing compensation events by using appropriate rates and lump sums as a basis, but this can only be done by agreement between the *Supply Manager* and the *Supplier*.

The *Supply Manager*'s 64
assessments 64.1 The four circumstances in which the *Supply Manager* assesses a compensation event are stated. They are all derived from some failure of the *Supplier*. In making his assessments, the *Supply Manager* will be motivated to make a fair and reasonable assessment in the knowledge that the *Supplier* may refer the matter to the *Adjudicator*, who may change the assessment.

64.3 This clause provides the *Supply Manager* with the same time to make his assessment as the *Supplier* was allowed for his assessment.

64.4 The procedure in this clause is designed to deal with a situation where the *Supply Manager* does not assess a compensation event within the time stated in the contract or a longer agreed time. The *Supplier* may notify the *Supply Manager* accordingly, which effectively provides the *Supply Manager* with a two week 'period of grace' to respond. If this produces no action from the *Supply Manager*, the quotation submitted by the *Supplier* is treated as having been accepted.

Implementing 65
compensation events 65.2 This clause emphasises the finality of the assessment of compensation events. If the records of resources on work actually carried out show that achieved Defined Cost is different from the forecast included in the accepted quotation or in the *Supply Manager*'s assessment, the assessment is not changed.

7 Title

CORE CLAUSES

Suppliers may be reluctant to pass title to their goods until they have been paid for. On the other hand purchasers may also be reluctant to pay for the goods until they are satisfied the supplier can pass title absolutely in return for their payment. The title clauses in the SC are drafted to accommodate both requirements.

If the delivery place is the *Purchaser*'s premises the *Supplier* may be prepared to hand over the *goods* and apply for payment. The *Supply Manager* then includes the *goods* for payment in his assessment of the amount due at the next assessment date. The *Purchaser* pays for them within three weeks of the assessment date unless stated otherwise in the Contract Data. The *Supplier* is only providing credit for a typical 30 day period.

However, if the Supply Requirements specify that the delivery place for the *goods* is alongside a ship at a port in the *Supplier*'s country and that the *goods* are then to be shipped to another continent by agents of the *Purchaser*, the *Supplier* may require payment for the *goods* before handing over the *goods* to the *Purchaser*'s agent. In this case the *Supplier* is required to mark the *goods* as the Goods Information requires. This is to minimise the *Purchaser*'s risk of title related problems that could possibly arise during transportation of the *goods* to the *Purchaser*'s final destination for the *goods*.

Matters of title, particularly in international transactions are complex and users of the SC are advised to seek expert legal advice on these matters where necessary.

The *Purchaser*'s title to the *goods* **70**

70.1 Because the SC may be used for high value international transactions the default position regarding title to the *goods* is that it should pass when the *goods* are paid for as the contract requires, rather than on Delivery.

To meet the requirements of this clause the Parties have the flexibility to use various methods of payment including stage payment and the use of documentary credit arrangements.

70.2 As an assurance for the *Purchaser*, the *Supplier* is obligated to provide information to the *Purchaser* showing that he either already has or is able to pass title absolutely before the payment is made.

Marking *goods* before Delivery **71**

71.1 If payment is to be made before the *goods* are brought to the delivery place, the *Supplier* marks them as the Goods Information requires. The Goods Information must identify the items as being subject to marking under the contract and state how the marking is to be done, listing any documentation that may also be required. Typical practice would be to label the *goods* with a statement that they are the property of the *Purchaser* in terms of the contract. A separate item could be included in the Price Schedule for this activity. The Goods Information should state not only how the *Supplier* is to mark the *goods* but also how the marking will be verified to the *Supply Manager* before payment is processed.

8 Risks, liabilities, indemnities and insurance

CORE CLAUSES

It is important to recognise the distinction between the various types of risk and which party bears them. Risks of loss of or physical damage to property or of personal injury or death, which are usually insurable risks, are quite separate from general, legal or financial risks.

The clauses in this section deal with the general, legal and the insurable risks of loss, damage, injury or death and what insurances are required to cover them. The risks which could result in loss, damage, injury or death, if they happen, are allocated to either the *Purchaser* or the *Supplier*.

Financial risks are dealt with in clause 88 (limits of liability) and in other parts of the contract, such as under the compensation event procedure in section 6. For example, the *Purchaser* carries the financial risk for additional work instructed under clause 60.1(1) but the risk in carrying it out remains with the *Supplier*. In addition, the *Purchaser* carries the financial risk if any events that are at his risk occur – see clause 60.1(12).

On the other hand, the *Supplier* carries the financial risk of doing work which he has priced in the contract.

Purchaser's risks 80

80.1   The *Purchaser*'s risks are stated in clause 80.1. There are four main categories of *Purchaser*'s risks.

The first is the *Purchaser*'s risks relating to the outcome of the supply of the *goods* and *services*, his own general or legal responsibilities and faults in any design he may have done of the *goods* and *services*. For liabilities which might arise from design faults, the *Purchaser* should either insure the risk if the design is by his own resources or ensure that it is covered under another contract if an external organisation is engaged to do the design work.

The second category, relating to plant and materials supplied to the *Supplier* by the *Purchaser*, is at the risk of the *Purchaser* up to the point of their handover to the *Supplier* or his Subcontractor. Any insurance cover for these items should be either under the *Purchaser*'s own loss or damage policy or the insurances of Others (as defined in clause 11.2(9)) until the *Supplier* or Subcontractor has received and accepted the plant and materials concerned. The process of receipt and acceptance should be documented to minimise disputes about the exact point when the risk passes from the one Party to the other.

The third and fourth categories of *Purchaser*'s risk is the loss of or damage to the *goods* and *services* after Delivery and any retained by the *Purchaser* if a termination occurs after Delivery. There are some important risks which, even after Delivery, remain with the *Supplier*, but these are likely to be small and cease at the *defects date*.

The last category of the *Purchaser*'s risks provides for him to carry additional risks. These must be clearly stated in the Contract Data.

An example of where the *Purchaser* might wish to carry an additional risk or limit the *Supplier*'s risk is when the *goods* are stored by the *Supplier* before Delivery to suit shipping timetables or a phased supply required by the *Purchaser*. Delivery only occurs in this case once the *goods* are taken from the *Supplier*'s store and transported to the delivery place stated in the Supply Requirements. Another example would be, in the case where the delivery place is inside the *Purchaser*'s property (say a refinery) and the *Purchaser* prefers to carry the risk of damage to his property which arises from the activities of the *Supplier*, such as unloading and using the *Purchaser*'s cranes to do so.

The *Supplier*'s risks 81

81.1 The *Supplier*'s risks are defined as all the risks which are not identified in clause 80.1 as being carried by the *Purchaser*. At first reading this looks like a daunting prospect for the *Supplier*, but in reality is no different to the risks he always carries in the course of his business, unless he excludes certain risks expressly. In any case the majority of risk is passed to the *Purchaser* at Delivery.

**Loss of and damage to 82
the *goods* 82.1** The *Supplier* is required to carry out all activities of repair to the *goods* until the *defects date*. Consequently, unless otherwise instructed by the *Supply Manager*, this will include repairs arising from a *Purchaser*'s risk event, such as damage to the *goods* after Delivery but before the *defects date*. The carrying out of such work will be a compensation event – see clause 60.1(12).

The *Supply Manager* must therefore decide how to deal with loss or damage caused by a *Purchaser*'s risk event. It is possible that, in certain circumstances, he decides the damage should not be repaired, or should be repaired by the *Purchaser* or others employed by him. In such a case he would issue instructions to the *Supplier*, who will then neither be obliged to carry out such repair activities nor be entitled to receive any compensation.

Indemnity 83

83.1 Under this clause each Party indemnifies the other for events which are at his risk. This includes all types of risk as identified above.

83.2 Provision is made for the liability of a Party to be reduced on a proportional basis if events at the risk of the other Party contributed to the event.

Insurance cover 84

84.1 This clause requires the *Supplier* to take out insurance cover to the extent stated in the Insurance Table, except for any insurance which the *Purchaser* provides.

Major multi-discipline purchasers may prefer to arrange all or some of this insurance themselves in view of the large number and size of contracts in which they invest. If the *Purchaser* wishes to effect his own insurance, the details should be given in the Contract Data. However the *Supplier* needs to understand the extent of cover which the *Purchaser* provides as it may not be the cover required by the right hand column of the Insurance Table, leaving the *Supplier* to insure the balance up to the limits stated.

84.2 The Insurance Table lists the categories of insurance and the minimum amount of cover required.

The first category of insurance is against the *Supplier*'s risks of loss of or damage to the *goods* and any plant and materials essentially until Delivery plus cover for the exceptions listed in clause 80.1, third main bullet. It therefore includes a provision for cover of any plant and materials provided by the *Purchaser* to the *Supplier*.

The second category of insurance is against loss of or damage to property (including the *Purchaser*'s) and injury to or death of a person not employed by the *Supplier*. This is typically third party insurance.

The third category of insurance relates to the *Supplier*'s own employees which in many countries is required by law.

These statements of insurance requirements are broad and designed to cover most common practices as well as provide the Parties with a structured approach to insurance if circumstances require it. If users make use of Incoterms in the Supply Requirements they will find that the insurance obligations within the chosen Incoterm fit within the first category in the Insurance Table.

The complexities of freight and marine insurance are beyond the scope of these Guidance Notes and users of the SC should always seek the necessary expert advice for these insurances.

It is also important to note that the insurances in the Insurance Table only cover for events which are at the *Supplier*'s risk. Thus, whilst the insurances run until the *defects date*, the *Purchaser* assumes most of the risks for the *goods* after Delivery and therefore the *goods* will not be covered by this insurance.

Insurance policies 85

85.1   The *Supply Manager* has the option of requesting the *Supplier* to provide certificates for his acceptance confirming that the required insurances are in place.

If the *Supply Manager* is not an expert in insurances he may need to consult an insurance expert or refer the matter to the *Purchaser*'s insurance department.

85.2   The purpose of waiver of subrogation rights is to prevent insurers taking action against the *Purchaser*'s personnel, for example after having paid money to the *Supplier* in settlement of a claim by him.

85.3   The Parties must comply with the terms of the insurance policies as not so to do may make the insurance partially or fully void and incur the Parties in substantial risk. It is therefore important that the *Supply Manager* is aware of any terms that may affect, or be affected by, the actions of the *Purchaser*.

This clause is referring in particular to 'deductibles'. Deductibles, often also known as 'excesses', represent the amount of liability retained by the insured. By this means, the insured shares the exposure to risk with the insurer.

The amount of the deductible affects the level of premium which the insured must pay. Reasons for applying deductibles in insurance policies include

- decrease in level of premiums,
- elimination of administration costs of processing a large number of small claims,
- involving the insured in retaining some liability by sharing the risks and thus encouraging him to take more care in avoiding loss or damage,
- reducing the risk assumed by the insurer to a limit which he can bear.

**If the *Supplier* does 86
not insure**

86.1   This clause enables the *Purchaser* to take out the relevant insurances in the event that the *Supplier* fails to do so at the time and for the periods stated in the contract. Appropriate adjustments are then made to the amounts certified by the *Supply Manager*.

**Insurance by the 87
*Purchaser***

87.1   Although not common practice in supply contracts, in certain circumstances it may be more appropriate and convenient for the *Purchaser* to affect some of the insurances which, under the standard conditions of contract, are to be taken out by the *Supplier*. The *Supplier* is required to accept the policies and certificates, in the same way that the *Purchaser* is required to do so for insurances effected by the *Supplier*.

The *Purchaser* sets out details of the insurances that he is going to effect, including the deductibles applicable. If in doubt, the *Purchaser* should discuss the level of deductibles with potential tenderers before completing the Contract Data.

Entering 'nil' or very low amounts against the deductibles in the Contract Data will normally not be in the *Purchaser*'s best interests because the premiums will be very high. Conversely, high levels of deductibles may lead tenderers to seek to insure all or part of the deductible amount, and either increasing their bid to cover additional premiums or qualifying their tender if they are unable to obtain suitable additional cover.

Tenderers will do this because the insured risks are *Supplier*'s risks and therefore the *Supplier* will bear the cost of the deductibles regardless of who effects the policies.

87.2 Whilst the *Supplier* is entitled to rely upon the *Purchaser* providing the insurances as stated in the Contract Data, it is important that the *Supplier* recognises that his risks include those shown in the Insurance Table. Consequently, even if such insurances are effected by the *Purchaser*, the *Supplier* should satisfy himself as to the adequacy of the policy and cover. The *Supplier* should inform the *Supply Manager* of any discrepancy between the *Purchaser* provided insurances as stated in the Contract Data and the *Purchaser*-provided insurances as actually given and ask for a policy amendment.

87.3 If the *Purchaser* fails to effect the insurances which the Contract Data states he is to provide, or provides insurances which do not comply with the Contract Data, the *Supplier* may procure additional insurance to top up any shortfall he considers exists in these insurances. The *Purchaser* will then either pay the insurers directly or the *Supplier* will be reimbursed.

Limitation of liability

This clause places limits on various liabilities that the *Supplier* may have to the *Purchaser* arising under or in connection with the contract. It is particularly relevant to international transactions because of the uncertain position which suppliers could face in some jurisdictions regarding their liabilities. This clause addresses three key liabilities. It can also provide overall caps, in terms of both time and money, beyond which the *Supplier* has no further liability to the *Purchaser*.

Flexibility has been maintained by the use of amounts stated in the Contract Data for each cap, which can vary from 'nil' to whatever amount the Parties are prepared to accept. If the *Purchaser* wants to use some, but not all, of the provisions of this clause he can insert the word 'unlimited' against those matters that he does not wish to cap.

Users are advised to seek legal advice relating to the law under which the contract is to be made in order to be aware of how these provisions and the amounts used may be applied under that law.

88.1 This clause limits the *Supplier*'s exposure to what are commonly referred to as consequential or indirect losses incurred by the *Purchaser*.

88.2 If the *Supplier* is required to work within or adjacent to the *Purchaser*'s facility, such as when unloading *goods* or commissioning the *goods* as part of the *services*, the *Supplier* is exposed to risks arising from damage he may cause to such a facility. The *Purchaser*'s costs arising from such an incident could be many times greater than the value of the contract, or of the insurance which either Party may have arranged either under the contract or otherwise. This clause limits the claim the *Purchaser* may make against the *Supplier* for his costs.

The amount stated in Contract Data would typically be set to something within the amount of cover provided by the insurance if the *Supplier* provides the insurance or closer to the deductible if the *Purchaser* provides the insurance. However, the *Purchaser* should check with their insurers first in case the insurer advises the *Purchaser* to set the amount at a higher level to retain rights of subrogation.

88.3 The *Supplier*'s liability for his design can be limited to an amount stated in the Contract Data. The *Supplier*'s obligation is to design strictly in compliance with the Goods Information. In English law, for example, the *Supplier* would be responsible for ensuring that his design is fit for the purpose stated in or reasonably implied from the Goods Information.

Clause 45.1 covers the cost of correcting any uncorrected Defects notified before the *defects date*. The limited liability for the *Supplier*'s design has effect only for Defects notified after the last *defects date* sometimes referred to as latent defects.

The term 'design' is generally interpreted in the broadest sense. It may include not merely design calculations and the dimensions, shape and function of the *goods*, but also the choice of particular plant and materials for particular functions and, similarly, the choice of particular manufacturing processes.

88.4   This clause limits the *Supplier*'s overall liability to the *Purchaser* to an amount stated in the Contract Data, subject to the exclusions stated. The amount stated should be equal to or higher than the other limiting amounts stated elsewhere in this clause to allow for amounts that may become due to the *Purchaser* from other rights he may have under the applicable law.

This clause also confirms that the limits apply irrespective of whether the *Purchaser* is making the claim under the contract, in tort (or delict in some jurisdictions) or in terms of any other right the *Purchaser* might have under the *law of the contract*.

Amounts payable by the *Supplier* for the listed excluded matters are not included within this limit. However, although loss and damage to the *Purchaser*'s property is listed as an exclusion, this can, nevertheless, be limited under clause 88.2.

88.5   In law the *Supplier*'s liability to the *Purchaser* may not end at the last *defects date* particularly for a Defect or other matter which only becomes apparent some time after the *defects date*. Such Defects are often referred to as latent defects. Many, but not all, legal jurisdictions have cut-off periods after which the *Supplier* is no longer liable for such latent defects or any other matters under the contract. Clause 88.5 can be used to either reduce the cut-off period set by law or, if none exists, add such a cut-off period.

The *Supplier* is not liable to the *Purchaser* for any matter, which would include any Defect, which is notified to him after the *end of liability date*.

9 Termination and dispute resolution

CORE CLAUSES

The clauses in this section describe the circumstances under which the Parties may terminate and the subsequent procedures on termination and the procedures for dispute resolution.

Termination 90

90.1   Both the *Purchaser* and *Supplier* have rights to terminate the *Supplier*'s obligations under the contract in certain circumstances. This termination does not terminate the contract itself. The Party wishing to terminate initiates the procedure by notifying the *Supply Manager* and giving his reasons for terminating. If satisfied that the Party giving notice has provided reasons which are valid under the contract, the *Supply Manager* issues a termination certificate promptly.

It is important to note that these clauses confer rights on to the Parties, but it is not mandatory that those rights are exercised.

90.2   Only the *Purchaser* has a right of termination entirely at his discretion, i.e. without one of the reasons listed in clause 91 as R1 to R21. The *Supplier* can terminate only for one of the reasons listed in the Termination Table. The reasons are given identification references (R1 to R21) for convenience and are fully described in clause 91. If the *Purchaser* wishes to terminate for a reason other than those in R1 to R21, he should state this in notifying the *Supply Manager* under clause 90.1.

The procedures to be followed and the amount due to the *Supplier* are generally functions of the reasons for terminating, although some are independent of the reasons.

90.3   The procedures to be followed on termination are given in clause 92.

90.4   Details of the amount to be paid to or by the *Supplier* after termination are given in clause 93 in conjunction with the Termination Table. The *Supply Manager* is required to carry out his assessment of the amount due so that he can certify the final payment within thirteen weeks. The *Purchaser* pays the *Supplier* any sums certified by the *Supply Manager* within three weeks of them being certified. If the sum is due to the *Purchaser* from the *Supplier* the same time limit applies.

Reasons for termination 91

91.1   The reasons set out in clause 91.1 deal with bankruptcy of either Party. The terminology of bankruptcy law varies from country to country. The terms used in this clause are those current in English law but the clause allows for equivalents in other jurisdictions. Termination may follow the bankruptcy, etc., of either the *Supplier* or the *Purchaser*.

The exercise of the right to termination when either Party is faced with the bankruptcy, etc. is not mandatory. For example, it may be in the best interests of the *Purchaser*, when first hearing of the matter to discuss with the receiver, administrator or liquidator the possibility of the *Supplier* completing his obligations or being able to novate the contract to a third party such that the supply can continue with a minimum of disruption.

91.2   The four week period of grace is provided so that the *Supplier* has the opportunity to correct the default. Notification should be issued to the *Supplier* and usually copied to the *Purchaser*. If after four weeks the *Supplier* has not corrected the default, the *Supply Manager* would, by implication, need to advise the *Purchaser* of the position so that the *Purchaser* can exercise his right if he wishes. The *Supplier* may have started to make amends but not fully corrected the default after the four week period. In this case, the *Purchaser* will need to decide whether or not he wishes to proceed to termination.

Reason R11 applies only to a substantial breach of the *Supplier*'s obligations. Minor breaches are insufficient grounds for the serious step of termination, as a matter of policy.

The guarantee in Option X4 and the bond in Option X13 are both to be provided within stated times. This clause effectively extends those times by four weeks. No time limits are given for providing an advance payment bond under Option X14. However, since this bond is provided as security against the advanced payment, delay in providing the bond merely delays the advanced payment to the *Supplier*, which is sufficient sanction.

Subcontracting of work before acceptance by the *Supply Manager* (R13) is breach of clause 26.2. However, the right to termination only arises when substantial work is subcontracted before acceptance of the Subcontractor.

It is important to note that it is for the *Purchaser* to decide if he wishes to terminate the *Supplier*'s obligation to provide the Goods and Services because of this default.

91.3 Both of these reasons include the word 'substantially' since minor defaults of this nature would not be sufficient grounds for termination. The right to termination for breach of a health and safety regulation is additional to any sanctions which may exist under the applicable law.

91.4 Late payment entitles the payee to interest under clause 51.2. The right to termination, however, only arises if payment by the *Purchaser* of an amount due to the *Supplier* is delayed beyond 11 weeks after the date it was due to be paid. This right can only be exercised by the *Supplier*.

91.5 Rights to terminate under the law (R17) may be the result, in some jurisdictions, of force majeure or frustration. In the event of a national emergency, such as declaration of war, a government often legislates to deal with existing contracts.

91.6 These reasons apply to instructions which relate to substantial or all work. Judgement is needed to interpret what constitutes substantial work. Procedures and payment depend on which Party was responsible for the default which led to the instruction. R20 provides for an instruction which resulted from the default of neither Party.

91.7 This reason is in effect recognition of a possible effect of force majeure, which is in any case limited in the SC. (See explanatory notes on clause 19). The event may have been notified under clause 16 or otherwise and, once recognised as satisfying the criteria set out in clause 19.1, it will have to be managed by the *Supply Manager*. The *Purchaser* now has the option to terminate if the event will prevent Delivery or is forecast to delay it by more than thirteen weeks.

Note that initially the event may have been notified as a compensation event under clause 60.1(12) and only recognised as a "force majeure" event when the *Supply Manager* and the *Supplier* consider how to deal with it.

Procedures on termination 92

92.1 This clause provides flexibility to the *Purchaser* on termination to decide how and if the remaining *goods* and *services* are to be obtained. It applies irrespective of the terminating party or the reasons for termination. The *Purchaser* may have to decide the benefit to him and the need of part finished *goods* and negotiate with the administrator for the benefit of reduced liability.

92.2 Under procedure P2, the *Purchaser*'s right to enforce assignment of the benefits of a subcontract will be subject to the terms of the subcontract. In certain cases, a new contract (novation) may be necessary.

Procedure P3 is particularly useful to a *Purchaser* where there are substantial items of equipment involved in the supply of the *goods* and *services*. However it can only apply to equipment that the *Supplier* has title to. Equipment which is being hired by the *Supplier* or which is owned by a subcontractor cannot be dealt with in this way unless the *Supplier* has obtained title to it. In that case the *Purchaser* could use procedure P2, if available. Otherwise he will be required to negotiate with the equipment's owner for it's continued use.

Title to any equipment retained by the *Purchaser* remains with the *Supplier*. The *Purchaser* is only allowed to use the equipment to complete the supply of the *goods* and *services* and cannot retain it for other use or sell it or dispose of it once he no longer needs it. The *Supplier* is required to remove the equipment retained by the *Purchaser* once it is no longer required to supply the *goods* and *services*.

Payment on termination 93

93.1 The amounts listed in this clause (A1) are due whatever the reason for the termination.

When paying the Defined Cost care must be taken to ensure that there is no duplication with any amount that is assessed as being due for normal payments. For example, the Defined Cost paid in addition to normal payments must not be used to recover losses due to underestimates in the Prices used to assess normal payments for items already delivered.

Defined Cost that the *Supplier* has reasonably incurred in expectation of completing the supply of the *goods* and *services* should include costs which the *Supplier* can show has not been recovered within the normal amount due. For example, it would include amounts for the work done to the date of termination on items included in the Price Schedule which were not completed at that time.

93.2 The applicability of these amounts (A2 and A3) depends on the particular grounds of termination. Generally, where termination occurs because of the *Supplier*'s default, the *Supplier* is not reimbursed the cost of removing his equipment. He must also pay the *Purchaser*'s additional costs for providing the whole of the *goods* and *services*, representing at least some of the damages which the *Purchaser* suffers arising from the *Supplier*'s breach of contract.

Dispute resolution 94

94.1 Disputes are to be dealt with by adjudication in the first instance.

The dispute resolution process should not be seen as an alternative to the Parties reaching agreement on their disputes, either through informal negotiation, or via other more formal non-binding processes such as mediation or conciliation. Such negotiations will usually need to take place within a short time period if Option W1 is used, because of the limited time available to refer a dispute to the *Adjudicator* in that Option. However the Parties are free to agree to extend the time limits set out in W1, in accordance with clause W1.3(2), if they feel that more time is needed for resolving the dispute. If either the notification or the referral is not made within the time stated or extended by agreement, the Parties may no longer dispute the matter.

The *Adjudicator* 94.2

(1) The person appointed as *Adjudicator* is named in part one of the Contract Data. He is to be appointed jointly by the Parties using the NEC *Adjudicator*'s Contract (one of the NEC family of standard contracts published by Thomas Telford, London). His fees are shared equally between the Parties to a dispute, regardless of his decision, unless otherwise agreed.

The *Adjudicator* should be a person with experience of the kind of *goods* and *services* required of the *Supplier* and who occupies or has occupied a senior position dealing with similar dispute problems. He should be able to understand the point of view of both *Purchaser* and *Supplier* and to judge the required level of competence, and be able to act impartially.

(2) The obligation of impartiality is fundamental to the role of *Adjudicator*. The duty is repeated in the NEC Adjudicator's Contract. The *Adjudicator*'s status is different from that of an arbitrator.

(3)   In accordance with the Parties' basic obligations under clause 10.1 they are required to try and agree the *Adjudicator*. The *Adjudicator* is appointed jointly by the *Purchaser* and the *Supplier* for the contract. The *Purchaser* should insert his choice of *Adjudicator* in part one of the Contract Data. If the *Supplier* does not agree with the choice, a suitable person will be the subject of discussion and agreement before the Contract Date. Alternatively, the *Purchaser* may propose a list of acceptable names and the *Supplier* may be asked to select one of them to be *Adjudicator*. Some *Purchaser*s may prefer the *Supplier* to propose suitable names.

Where an *Adjudicator* has not been named in the Contract Data, this clause describes the procedure for appointing one. The procedure also applies where a replacement adjudicator is needed in the event that the named *Adjudicator* is unable to act. In the United Kingdom there are several *Adjudicator* nominating bodies, which are able to appoint a suitable person as *Adjudicator*.

(4)   An existing dispute on which the original *Adjudicator* has not made a decision are automatically referred to the replacement adjudicator. It is important that the Parties ensure that the replacement adjudicator receives all relevant information. The time stated in the contract for supply of information then runs from the time of appointment of the replacement adjudicator.

If a need arises for a temporary replacement adjudicator (e.g. during the *Adjudicator*'s holiday), the Parties should agree a temporary appointment.

(5)   It is important that the person appointed as *Adjudicator* is protected from legal actions by the Parties and others.

The adjudication 94.3
(1)   This clause sets out in the Adjudication Table the procedure and timetable for the referral of various types of dispute to the *Adjudicator*.

The first item in the table deals with a disputed action of the *Supply Manager* and the second item deals with his lack of action. The third item deals with the situation that may occur under clauses 62.6 or 64.4 whereby failure by the *Supply Manager* to properly administer the assessment of a compensation event in accordance with the contract may lead to a *Supplier*'s quotation being treated as accepted. Under this item, if the *Purchaser* disagrees with the quotation, he may refer it to the *Adjudicator* but only within the time limits stated. The fourth item deals with all other disputes.

The action in dispute under the first item may be for example

- an instruction,
- an acceptance, non-acceptance or rejection,
- a certification,
- an assessment,
- a notification,
- a decision.

Each of these is a separate action or lack of action.

For a general matter in dispute, either Party may submit it to the *Adjudicator*. For matters concerning an action or lack of action by the *Supply Manager* only the *Supplier* is permitted to submit it to the *Adjudicator*. This is because at all times the *Supply Manager* is acting on behalf of the *Purchaser*. The only exception to this is the third item in the table; in this case only the *Purchaser* may refer the dispute.

The initial period of two weeks after the *Supplier*'s notification gives the *Supply Manager* the opportunity to take or amend the action. This period of grace is intended to prevent the *Adjudicator* becoming involved in matters which may have been overlooked.

(2)   Times stipulations are clearly set out in the Adjudication Table in order to avoid protracted exchanges and argument and to achieve prompt resolution of disputes. However, some disputes can be complex and the times stated may be inappropriate. In that case and in other cases where the Parties are continuing to negotiate a settlement of the dispute, they should agree to extend the periods set out in the table.

The final sentence of this clause makes the time periods set out in the Adjudication Table, or subsequently extended, time barring. If they are not met, the Parties loose the right to refer the disputed matter to the *Adjudicator*, and also, because of clause 94.1(1) to the *tribunal*.

(3)   It is important that the *Adjudicator* has all the relevant information to enable him to reach his decision. The Party referring the dispute is required to include full information about the dispute. The other Parties are required to submit all of their information within a further four weeks, or such other longer period as may be decided by the *Adjudicator*.

(4)   Where a dispute which affects work which has been subcontracted arises, and which may constitute a dispute between the *Supplier* and a Subcontractor as well as between the *Supplier* and the *Purchaser*, there is provision for the matter to be resolved between the three parties by the main contract *Adjudicator*. This saves time and expense and prevents a dispute being dealt with by different adjudicators who may make different decisions. This procedure is only possible if the terms of the subcontract permit the *Supplier* to submit the subcontract dispute to the main contract *Adjudicator*.

(5)   The *Adjudicator* has wide powers to manage the adjudication and ensure that he has all of the information he needs to reach a fair decision on the dispute within the time limits set out in the contract. The *Adjudicator* must ensure that he uses these powers fairly and reasonably.

(6)   It is important that copies of the communications sent to the *Adjudicator* are sent to the other Party so that each Party is aware of the other Party's case.

(8)   This clause sets out the period in which the *Adjudicator* may reach his decision, and the circumstances under which it can be extended. In complex disputes, and for other valid reasons, the *Adjudicator* may require a period greater than the four weeks stated. For example, the *Adjudicator* may require time to visit the manufacturing facility and may need to consult with other people to help him in arriving at his decision. Consequently, whilst the extension of this period requires the agreement of the Parties, it is recommended that any extra time sought by the *Adjudicator* should be allowed.

(10)   The *Adjudicator*'s decision is binding upon the Parties and they are contractually obliged to act upon it. If they fail to do so it can usually be enforced in the courts, in the same way, and to the same extent, as any other contractual obligation. The *Adjudicator*'s decision becomes final as well as binding on the Parties if neither of them notifies the other within the time set out in clause 94.4(2) that he is dissatisfied with it and intends to refer it to the *tribunal*. Note this timescale only applies to the notification of intention to refer and not to the referral itself, which can, and normally will, take place later.

(11)   Once the *Adjudicator* has made his decision and notified it to the Parties his role in the dispute would normally be over. This clause gives him the right to subsequently correct any clerical errors or any ambiguities within a limited period. However, it does not enable him to change any important parts of his decision or the reasons and it cannot be used to re-open the decision.

Review by the *tribunal* 94.4

(1)   A dispute cannot be referred to the *tribunal* unless it has first been referred to the *Adjudicator*. If the *Adjudicator* does not decide the dispute, either at all or within the timescales in clause 93.3(8), the remedy for either Party is to ask the *tribunal* to decide the dispute, but they only have a limited period to do so – clause 94.4(3).

(2)   The effect of this clause is time-barring. If either Party is dissatisfied with the *Adjudicator*'s decision they have a short period to notify the other of their dissatisfaction. If neither Party does so within that period, the *Adjudicator*'s decision becomes final as well as binding and it can no longer be referred to the *tribunal*. The stated period is only for the notification of dissatisfaction. The dispute can be, and normally is, referred to the *tribunal* at a later date.

(3)   The effect of this clause is time-barring. If the *Adjudicator* does not decide the dispute within the time period set out in clause 93.3(8) then either Party has a further four weeks (from the date that the decision should have been given) to notify the other that they intend to refer the dispute to the *tribunal*. If neither Party does so within that period, the dispute cannot be referred to the *tribunal*. The stated period is only for the notification of the intention to refer the dispute to the *tribunal*. The dispute can be, and normally is, referred to the *tribunal* at a later date.

OPTION CLAUSES

Option X1: Price adjustment for inflation

The *Purchaser* should decide how the risk of inflation is to be allocated. If he decides to accept this risk himself, he should include Option X1. Without Option X1, the contract is firm price in terms of inflation uncertainty and the *Supplier* carries the risk of inflationary increases in the cost of labour, plant and materials, etc.

Use of this Option has the effect of largely transferring the risk of inflation during the period of the contract to the *Purchaser*. It uses the formula method. It is appropriate where inflation is high and likely to be variable throughout this period.

Where inflation is low and the period over which the contract is to take place is short, the risk may not be great. Thus, the *Supplier* should be able to assess the allowance for inflation in deciding the rates and prices in the Price Schedule.

Defined terms **X1**

X1.1 The source of the published priced indices to be used should be identified in part one of the Contract Data, together with the proportions of the total value of the *goods* and *services* to be linked to the index for each category. Allowance is made for a non-adjustable portion, which represents the portion for which the *Supplier* carries the risk of inflation. The non-adjustable portion is usually a small proportion of the total factor – a maximum of 10% is normally considered reasonable. The total of the proportions should be unity. Also entered in the Contract Data is the base date, which should normally be four to six weeks before the latest date for submitting tenders.

Price Adjustment Factor X1.2 Quite often, provisional index figures are published and these are corrected at a later date. This clause requires re-calculation using final figures where these are different from provisional figures.

Compensation events X1.3 Compensation events are assessed under clause 63. Where only quantities of work are affected by the compensation event, the rates in the Price Schedule are used (clause 63.1). These rates are at base date level. Other compensation events are assessed as the effect of the event on Defined Cost – either recorded past cost or forecast future cost, or a combination of the two. This assessment will be done using prices current at the date when the assessment is done. Clause X1.3 has the effect of reducing current Defined Cost to base date levels so that changes to the Prices for compensation events are made in base date terms.

When assessments of the amount due are made, the amount for completed items will be adjusted for inflation under clause X1.4.

If Option X1 is not included in a contract, the contract is fixed price with respect to inflation. However, compensation events are still assessed under clause 63, which in the general case will be a mixture of current costs and base date costs. Tenderers will need to consider the allowance for inflation in the rates in the Price Schedule as these may be used for assessing compensation events.

Price adjustment X1.4 'Each amount due' is the total to date and only the change in the amount due is payable (clause 51.1). Thus the total of the three bullet points listed in clause X1.4 represents the total amount in respect of price adjustment up to the date of each assessment.

Example

Assume the increase in the amount due in a monthly assessment is £5,000 and the Price Adjustment Factor (PAF) is 0.05 (i.e. 5% inflation since the base date). The calculation for the first bullet point in clause X1.4 is:

£5,000 × 0.05 = £250

The sum of £250, plus the total of the sums resulting from the same calculation in previous months, plus any correcting amount resulting from the third bullet point, is the amount for price adjustment included in the total amount due.

X2: Changes in the law

Changes in the law X2

X2.1   This clause removes from the *Supplier* the risk of changes in the law of the country stated in the Contract Data which occur after the Contract Date. In certain countries, such changes can have a dramatic effect on the *Supplier's* costs and on his ability to make progress. Only changes which affect the *Supplier's* costs are included. Thus changes of law affecting the following are not compensation events.

- Income tax or any other tax paid by employees.
- Corporation tax or any other charges on profit.

The Parties will need to agree, for international transactions, which countries law applies to their contract in terms of the risks involved respective to that country.

For the purposes of this clause, law would include a national or state statute, ordinance, decree, regulation and a bylaw of a local or other duly constituted authority or other delegated legislation.

The *Supplier* may notify the *Supply Manager* of a compensation event under this Option using the procedure in clause 61.3. He is most likely to do this when a change in the law has the effect of increasing the cost to him of Providing the Goods and Services. However, the clause is reciprocal in the sense that the *Purchaser* gains the benefit of a change in the law which reduces costs.

X3: Multiple currencies

Multiple currencies X3

X3.1   This Option is used when it is intended that payment to the *Supplier* should be made in more than one currency and that the risk of *exchange rate* changes should be carried by the *Purchaser*. The effect is that the *Supplier* is protected from the currency *exchange rate* changes which take place after a fixed date as they affect designated items or activities of the *Supplier's* work.

If an item or activity is to be paid for by the *Purchaser* in the *currency of this contract* and the *Supplier* chooses to pay for it, or part of it, in another currency, the *Supplier* carries the risk of changes in the *exchange rate*. Payment to the *Supplier* is not affected.

If, however, the total of the Prices at the Contract Date, which will be expressed in the *currency of this contract*, includes items identified as to be paid by the *Purchaser* to the *Supplier* in another currency, the *Purchaser* takes the risk of any movement in the *exchange rate* after the date of the published *exchange rates* stated in the Contract Data. This is achieved by listing the items in the Contract Data and fixing the *exchange rate* to be used for each currency relative to the *currency of this contract*. This ensures that the *Supplier* is paid the amount of the other currency which he has quoted for the item.

X4: Parent company guarantee

Parent company guarantee **X4** Where the *Supplier* is one of a group of companies, provision of a guarantee of the parent company should provide greater financial security for the *Purchaser*.

X4.1 Where a parent company guarantee is required by the *Purchaser* it should be provided by the Contract Date. If that is not achieved, a four week limit is provided as a fall-back. Failure to provide the guarantee within this period entitles the *Supply Manager* to notify the default under clause 91.2. If the *Supplier* does not provide the guarantee within a further four weeks, the *Purchaser* is entitled to terminate. The form of guarantee should be included in the Goods Information in part one of the Contract Data. If the *Purchaser* wishes specific provision for the *Supplier* to price the guarantee separately in his tender, an appropriate item should be included in the Price Schedule.

X7: Delay damages

Delay damages **X7** Delay damages are liquidated damages paid by the *Supplier* if he fails to supply the *goods* and *services* by the Delivery Date. It is recommended that this Option is included in most contracts. Under English law and some other legal systems, if it is not included, delay damages are 'at large' and the remedy open to the *Purchaser* if the *Supplier* fails to supply the *goods* and *services* by the Delivery Date is to bring an action for damages for the *Supplier*'s breach of contract. In this event, evidence of the actual damages suffered by the *Purchaser* is required.

The amount of delay damages should not exceed a genuine pre-estimate of the damage which the *Purchaser* will suffer as a result of the *Supplier*'s breach. They are described as delay damages in the NEC family of contracts as these are not the only liquidated damages. Others are low performance damages (Option X17) and interest for delayed payments in clause 51.2.

X7.1 Appropriate entries for delay damages should be made in the Contract Data. They may comprise loss of profit from a manufacturing facility, consequential losses due to delayed supply affecting work on a project carried out under another contract, or simply interest on the capital invested in the *goods* and *services* for the period during which the *Purchaser* has been deprived of their benefit. The *Purchaser* is advised to keep a record of the calculation. Damages greater than a genuine pre-estimate constitute a penalty and are not generally enforceable under English law.

If Option X7 is used and no entry or a 'nil' entry is made in the Contract Data, it is likely that the *Purchaser* will be unable to recover any damages if the *Supplier* fails to supply the *goods* and *services* by the Delivery Date.

X7.2 This clause protects the *Supplier* when he has paid delay damages and a later assessment of a compensation event results in a delay to the Delivery Date. This could occur when a compensation event arises at a late stage in the supply or if the *Adjudicator* or the *tribunal* changes the assessment of a compensation event and their decision is made after delay damages have been paid. The *Purchaser* is required to repay the overpayment of delay damages with interest.

X7.3 If the *Purchaser* has had the benefit of using part of the *goods* and *services* before Delivery it would be unfair to levy damages in the contract applicable to all of the *goods* and *services* if the *Supplier* subsequently supplied the rest of the *goods* and *services* late. The delay damages are therefore reduced in the proportion that the benefit of the used part of the *goods* and *services* has to the benefit of the whole *goods* and *services*. It is important to note that when calculating this proportion the actual (or assessed) benefits known at the time of the calculation should be used, not those assumed when the delay damages were originally calculated. This proportion is then applied to the original damages.

X12: Partnering

This Option is used for partnering between more than two parties working on the same purchase, project or projects or on the provision of services. The Option is included in all NEC contracts which each party has with the body which is paying for the work, *goods* and *services* or service. The parties who have this Option included in their contracts are intended to make up the partnering team. The Partnering Option does not, however, create a multi-party contract.

The purpose of the Option is to establish the NEC family as an effective contract basis for multi-party partnering. By linking this Option to other bi-party contracts, the NEC can be used

- when the *goods* and *services* are part of a major facility being constructed by others,
- for partnering for any number of purchases, projects and services,
- internationally,
- for purchases, projects and services of any technical composition and
- as far down the supply chain as required.

Parties must recognise that by entering into a contract which includes Option X12, they will be undertaking responsibilities additional to those in the basic NEC contract.

A dispute (or difference) between Partners who do not have a contract between themselves is resolved by the Core Group. This is the Group that manages the conduct of the Partners in accordance with the Partnering Information. If the Core Group is unable to resolve the issue, then it is resolved under the procedure of the Partners' individual contracts, either directly or indirectly with the Client who will always be involved at some stage in the contractual chain. The Client may seek to have issues on all contracts dealt with simultaneously.

The Partnering Option does not include direct remedies between non-contracting Partners to recover losses suffered by one of them caused by failure of the other. These remedies remain available in each Partner's individual contract, but their existence will encourage the parties to compromise any differences that arise. This applies to all levels of the supply chain, as a *Supplier* who is a Partner retains the responsibility for actions of a subcontractor who is a Partner. The final sanction against any Partner who fails to act as stated in the Partnering Option is for the Partner who employed them not to invite them to partner again.

There are many scenarios possible in which the Partnering Option may be used. The NEC family of contracts with the Partnering Option is sufficiently flexible to deal with them. For example, the contract may be an Engineering and Construction Contract or an Engineering and Construction Short Contract for a project. It may involve also a Supply Contract and a Professional Services Contract. Later, a Term Service Contract may cover maintenance of the asset created by the project and provision of *goods* and *services* and other services for the Client.

Identified and defined terms X12.1

(1) The point at which someone becomes a Partner is when his Own Contract (which includes the Partnering Option) comes into existence. They should be named in the Schedule of Partners, and their representative identified.

(3) Not every Partner is a member of the Core Group.

(5) There are two options for subcontractor partners. Either the amount payable cascades down if the schedule allocates the same bonus/cost to the Supplier and subcontractor, or the *Supplier* absorbs the bonus/cost and does not pass it on.

Working together X12.3

(5) The Core Group organises and holds meetings. It produces and distributes records of each meeting, which include agreed actions. Instructions from the Core Group are issued in accordance with the Partner's Own Contract. The Core Group may invite other Partners or people to attend a meeting of the Core Group.

(8) The Partners should give advice and assistance when asked, and in addition whenever they identify something that would be helpful to another Partner.

(9) A subcontractor may be a Partner, but the general policy on this should be decided at the beginning of the purchase, project or service contract. The Core Group should advise the *Supplier* at the outset if a subcontractor is to be asked to be a Partner. A subcontractor who the Core Group decides should be a Partner should not be appointed if he is unwilling to be a Partner.

Incentives X12.4

(1) If one Partner lets the others down for a particular purchase, project or service by poor performance, then all lose their bonus for that target. If the *Purchaser* tries to prevent a target being met, he is in breach of clause 10.1.

There can be more than one Key Performance Indicator (KPI) for each partner. KPI's may apply to one Partner, to several Partners or to all Partners.

Example of a KPI

KPI	Number of days to complete seating to each train carriage
Target	3 days
Measurement	Number of train carriages completed
Amount	Supplier £X per completion
	Seating subcontractor £Y per completion

(2) The Client should consult with the other Partners before adding a KPI. The effect on subcontracted work should be noted. Adding a KPI to *goods* and *services* or work which is subcontracted can involve a change to the KPI for a subcontractor.

Option X13: Performance bond

Performance bond X13

This Option requires the *Supplier* to provide a bond to secure his performance of the contract. It therefore provides some protection for the *Purchaser*. A *Purchaser* may elect not to include it if he has confidence in the *Supplier* and experience of his previous good performance.

X13.1 Where a performance bond is required by the *Purchaser* the ideal is that it should be provided by the Contract Date. If that is not achieved, a four week limit is provided as a fall-back. Failure to provide the bond within this period entitles the *Supply Manager* to notify the default under clause 91.2. If the *Supplier* does not provide the bond within a further four weeks, the *Purchaser* is entitled to terminate. The form of the performance bond should be included in the Goods Information and the amount of the bond should be stated in the

Contract Data. If the *Purchaser* wishes the *Supplier* to price the bond separately in his tender, an appropriate item should be included in the Price Schedule.

Option X14: Advanced payment to the *Supplier*

Advanced payment **X14**

X14.1 The option of making an advanced payment is intended for contracts in which the *Supplier* has to make a heavy investment at the beginning, for example to buy or mobilise major items of equipment before manufacturing work starts. The start time for repayment of the advanced payment and the repayment amounts are stated in part one of the Contract Data. It is advisable to set these data so that the advance is fully repaid within the first half of the supply period.

To ensure that an advanced payment is not duplicated, instructions to tenderers should make it clear that, when there is an advanced payment, the Price Schedule should not be priced to produce another advanced payment. For example, there should not be provision for early purchase of equipment in the Price Schedule if an advanced payment is to be made under this Option.

In entering the amount of the advanced payment in the Contract Data, it should be made clear whether the amount is inclusive or exclusive of VAT or other sales tax. If such tax is payable on amounts to be certified later by the *Supply Manager*, it would also be due on the advanced payments.

The advanced payment does not require an assessment to be made or certified by the *Supply Manager*. Instead, it imposes an obligation on the *Purchaser* to pay within the periods set out in X14.2. Some *Purchaser*'s or funding agencies' procedures require the production of a certificate by the *Supply Manager* before any payment can be made. If that is the case then the *Supply Manager* may need to assess and certify such payment, but that is not a requirement of the contract.

X14.2 This clause allows for the provision of a bond, if required by the *Purchaser*, as security for the advanced payment. The bond should normally be provided before the Contract Date, but if this is not achieved, the advanced payment can be delayed until not later than four weeks after the *Purchaser* has received the bond. The form of the bond should be included in the Goods Information by the *Purchaser*. The value of the bond decreases as the *Supplier* repays the advanced payment.

If the *Purchaser* wishes to make specific provision for the *Supplier* to price the bond in his tender, appropriate items should be included in the Price Schedule.

If the *Purchaser* is late in making the advanced payment, the financial consequences for the *Supplier* may be significant. For example, he may be unable to purchase or mobilise the equipment he needs, which could delay the supply and lead to him incurring additional costs. Therefore, the normal provision for interest due on late payments (clause 51.2) could be inappropriate and it is replaced by the assessment of the effects of the delay in making the advanced payment as a compensation event.

X14.3 The Contract Data should include the minimum number of weeks after the Contract Date after which the first instalment of the repayment of the advanced payment is included in the assessment. If the instalment is an amount, it should be a simple fraction of the amount of the advanced payment.

The advanced payment will normally be made before the first assessment of the amount due by the *Supply Manager* (clause 50.1). Repayment of the advanced payment takes place gradually as part of the certified payments of the amount due. A consequence of this is that the total of the certified payments made to the *Supplier* under the normal assessment procedure will always be less than the total payment (including the advanced payment) made to the *Supplier* when Option X14 is being used. This must always be borne in mind when including payments under the contract in the internal financial statements of the *Purchaser* and the *Supplier*.

Option X17: Low performance damages

Low performance **X17** This Option is used where the *goods* may not achieve the standards specified
damages in the Goods Information. In such cases the specified damages are payable by the *Supplier*.

X17.1 If the *Supplier* produces substandard *goods* and *services* the *Purchaser* can

- insist the *Supplier* corrects the Defect to provide the quality specified in the Goods Information (clause 43.1),
- recover the cost of having it corrected by other people if the *Supplier* fails to correct the Defect within the specified time (clause 45.1) or
- accept the Defect and also a quotation from the *Supplier* for reduced Prices, or an earlier Delivery Date, or both in return for a change to the Goods Information (clause 44).

Where the performance of the *goods* and *services* fails to reach the specified level due to a fault of the *Supplier* and the Defect is not or cannot be corrected, the *Purchaser* should be able to recover the damages he suffers in consequence. This Option provides for these damages to be recovered as liquidated damages. The required performance should be specified in the Goods Information.

The low performance damages included in the Contract Data should be a genuine pre-estimate of the actual damages that the *Purchaser* will suffer as a result of the *Supplier*'s breach. Under English law, damages greater than a genuine pre-estimate constitute a penalty and are not generally enforceable. The amount of damages is entered in the Contract Data part one against different ranges of low performance.

Option X20: Key Performance Indicators

X20.1 The performance of the *Supplier* can be monitored and measured against Key
to Performance Indicators (KPIs). Using this Option, KPIs are being increasingly
X20.5 used as a means of improving efficiency and encouraging better performance by a *Supplier* with a view to continuous improvement. Their aim is to offer an incentive to the *Supplier* to achieve the *Purchaser*'s objectives by setting clear measurable targets. These can be related to the *Purchaser*'s business wide or purchase specific objectives.

KPIs are provided for in Option X12 where partnering arrangements are in place. This Option X20 can be used when Option X12 is not used. The procedure in Option X20 requires the establishment of performance targets and regular reporting by the *Supplier* of his performance measured against the target KPIs.

Option Y(UK)1: Project Bank Account

Project Back Account   Y(UK)1
Y1.1

(1) The Option is used when the *Supplier* is included in the Project Bank Account (PBA) arrangements in the *Purchaser*'s contract with his employer.

The PBA is established and maintained by the *Purchaser*. Amounts due to the *Supplier* are paid into the Project Bank by the *Purchaser* and his employer, and payment to the *Supplier* is made by the Project Bank.

The Trust Deed is intended to allow payment to the *Supplier* to continue in the event of the insolvency of the *Purchaser*. The deed is executed by the *Purchaser* and his employer, the *Supplier* and other suppliers or subcontractors to the *Purchaser*. The *Supplier* will sign the Trust Deed when he has been identified in the *Purchaser*'s contract with his employer, or sign the Joining Deed if added later.

(2) and (3) The forms to be used for the Trust Deed and the Joining Deed are included in the SC. These forms must be included in the contract, placed after the entry in the Contract Data for Y1.1. The SC will oly be used as a sub-contract in the PBA arrangements, normally under the NEC3 Engineering and Construction Contract. If this were to be used under the NEC3 Term Service Contract (TSC), then refer to the TSC Contract and guidance notes for examples of the appropriate Trust Deed and the Joining Deed.

Option Y(UK)3: The Contracts (Rights of Third Parties) Act 1999

Third party rights   Y(UK)3
Y3.1

If it is decided to give rights under the contract to a third party, it is important that the rights are clearly stated in the Contract Data by reference to clauses in the *conditions of contract*.

Option Z: *Additional conditions of contract*

This Option should be used where the *Purchaser* wishes to include additional conditions. These should be carefully drafted in the same style as the core and optional clauses, using the same defined terms and other terminology. They should be carefully checked for consistency with the other conditions.

Additional conditions should be used only where absolutely necessary to accommodate special needs. The flexibility of the SC Options minimises the need for additional conditions. Additional conditions should never be used for matters which should properly be included in the Goods Information, e.g. constraints on how the *Supplier* is to Provide the Goods and Services. The important difference is that the Goods Information can be varied by the *Supply Manager* under clause 14.3 whereas information in the *conditions of contract* cannot be changed under the contract.

APPENDIX 1

Clause numbering system

1 General

Clause no.	Title	Clause no.
10	Actions	10.1
11	Identified and defined terms	11.1
		11.2(1) to (16)
12	Interpretation and the law	12.1 to 12.5
13	Communications	13.1 to 13.8
14	The *Supply Manager*	14.1 to 14.4
15	Disclosure	15.1
16	Early warning	16.1 to 16.4
17	Ambiguities and inconsistencies	17.1
18	Illegal and impossible requirements	18.1
19	Prevention	19.1

2 The *Supplier*'s main responsibilities

Clause no.	Title	Clause no.
20	Providing the Goods and Services	20.1
21	The *Supplier*'s design	21.1 to 21.3
22	Using the *Supplier*'s design and *services*	22.1
23	Working with the *Purchaser* and Others	23.1 to 23.2
24	Subcontracting	24.1 to 24.2
25	Other responsibilities	25.1 to 25.5

3 Time

Clause no.	Title	Clause no.
30	Starting and Delivery	30.1 to 30.2
31	The programme	31.1 to 31.3
32	Revising the programme	32.1 to 32.2
33	Access	33.1
34	Instructions to stop or not to start work	34.1
35	Acceleration	35.1 to 35.2

4 Testing and Defects

Clause no.	Title	Clause no.
40	Tests and inspections	40.1 to 40.6
41	Testing and inspection before Delivery	41.1
42	Searching for and notifying Defects	42.1 to 42.2
43	Correcting Defects	43.1 to 43.3
44	Accepting Defects	44.1 to 44.2
45	Uncorrected Defects	45.1 to 45.2

5 Payment

Clause no.	Title	Clause no.
50	Assessing the amount due	50.1 to 50.4
51	Payment	51.1 to 51.4
52	Defined Cost	52.1
53	The Price Schedule	53.1

6 Compensation events

Clause no.	Title	Clause no.
60	Compensation events	60.1(1) to (15)
61	Notifying compensation events	61.1 to 61.7
62	Quotations for compensation events	62.1 to 62.6
63	Assessing compensation events	63.1 to 63.12
64	The *Supply Manager*'s assessments	64.1 to 64.4
65	Implementing compensation events	65.1 to 65.3

7 Title

Clause no.	Title	Clause no.
70	The *Purchaser*'s title to the *goods*	70.1 to 70.2
71	Marking *goods* before Delivery	71.1

8 Risks, liabilities, indemnities and insurance

Clause no.	Title	Clause no.
80	*Purchaser*'s risks	80.1
81	The *Supplier*'s risks	81.1
82	Loss of and damage to the *goods*	82.1
83	Indemnity	83.1 to 83.2
84	Insurance cover	84.1 to 84.2
85	Insurance policies	85.1 to 85.4
86	If the *Supplier* does not insure	86.1
87	Insurance by the *Purchaser*	87.1 to 87.3
88	Limitation of liability	88.1 to 88.5

9 Termination and dispute resolution

Clause no.	Title	Clause no.
90	Termination	90.1 to 90.5
91	Reasons for termination	91.1 to 91.7
92	Procedures on termination	92.1 to 92.2
93	Payment on termination	93.1 to 93.2
94	Dispute resolution	94.1
	The *Adjudicator*	94.2(1) to (5)
	The adjudication	94.3(1) to (11)
	Review by the *tribunal*	94.4(1) to (6)

Option clauses

Clause no.	Option	Title	Clause no.
X1	Price adjustment for inflation	Defined terms Price Adjustment Factor Compensation events Price adjustment	X1.1(a) to (c) X1.2 X1.3 X1.4
X2	Changes in the law	Changes in the law	X2.1
X3	Multiple currencies	Multiple currencies	X3.1 to X3.2
X4	Parent company guarantee	Parent company guarantee	X4.1
X7	Delay damages	Delay damages	X7.1 to X7.3
X12	Partnering	Identified and defined terms Actions Working together Incentives	X12.1(1) to (5) X12.2(1) to (6) X12.3(1) to (9) X12.4(1) to (2)
X13	Performance bond	Performance bond	X13.1
X14	Advanced payment to the *Supplier*	Advanced payment	X14.1 to X14.3
X17	Low performance damages	Low performance damages	X17.1
X20	Key Performance Indicators (not used with Option X12)	Incentives	X20.1 to X20.5
Y(UK)1	Project Back Account	Project Back Account	Y1.1 to Y1.6
Y(UK)3	The Contracts (Rights of Third Parties) Act 1999	Third party rights	Y3.1
Z	*Additional conditions of contract*	*Additional conditions of contract*	Z1.1

APPENDIX 2

Sample form of tender

TENDER

The *goods* and *services* . . . .

To. . . . . (the *Purchaser*)

Address . . . .

. . . .

. . . .

. . . .

We offer to Provide the Goods and Services in accordance with the Contract Data part one and the attached Contract Data part two for a sum to be determined in accordance with the *conditions of contract*.

You may accept this offer on or before [date of last day for acceptance].

Yours faithfully,

Signed . . . .

Name. . . . .

Position . . . .

On behalf of. . . . .(the *Supplier*)

Address . . . .

. . . .

. . . .

. . . .

Date. . . . .

APPENDIX 3

Sample form of agreement

This agreement is made on the . . . . day of . . . . 20 . . . . between

• . . . .

  of . . . .

  . . . .(the *Purchaser*) and

• . . . .

  of . . . .

  . . . .(the *Supplier*)

The *Purchaser* wishes to have the following *goods* and *services* provided

. . . .

. . . .

. . . .

1 The *Supplier* will Provide the Goods and Services in accordance with the *conditions of contract* identified in the Contract Data.

2 The *Purchaser* will pay the *Supplier* the amount due, and carry out his duties in accordance with the *conditions of contract* identified in the Contract Data.

3 The documents forming part of this agreement are

   • the *Supplier*'s tender
   • the *Purchaser*'s letter of acceptance
   • the Price Schedule
   • the Contract Data part one
   • the Contract Data part two
   • the following documents

. . . .

. . . .

. . . .

. . . .

. . . .

Signed by

Name . . . .

Position . . . .

On behalf of (*Purchaser*) . . . .

and

Name . . . .

Position . . . .

On behalf of (*Supplier*) . . . .

ALTERNATIVE IF AGREEMENT IF EXECUTED AS A DEED

Executed as a deed by the *Purchaser* (where the *Purchaser* is a company)

. . . .(name of Director)

. . . .(signature of Director)

. . . .(name of Director or Company Secretary)

. . . . (signature of Director or Company Secretary)

and as a deed by the *Supplier* (where the *Supplier* is a company)

. . . .(name of Director)

. . . .(signature of Director)

. . . .(name of Director or Company Secretary)

. . . . (signature of Director or Company Secretary)

APPENDIX 4

Use of the SC as a subcontract

The SC can be used as a subcontract to the SC or other contracts from the NEC family. If so, it will need to be adapted as suggested in the following notes, which should be read in conjunction with the main guidance notes.

Options

Use of the SC as a subcontract ensures as far as possible that the two contracts are 'back-to-back'. This minimises the risk to the *Supplier* as he passes his risks to the Subcontractor in respect of the work in the subcontract. If the SC is used as a subcontract to the SC the payment mechanism is 'back-to-back'. However, it is possible that the *Supplier* may be appointed as a subcontractor to a main contractor (Purchaser) who is appointed under another NEC contract (for example the ECC). The main Option in the ECC main contract may be different to the payment mechanism in the SC. For example, the ECC main contract may be carried out under Option C. This will affect such things as payment and assessment of compensation events (see below).

Identification of terms

When using the SC as a subcontract to the SC, the *Purchaser* named in the Contract Data for the subcontract would be the *Supplier* in the main contract. The *Supplier* named in the subcontract would be the Supplier (Y) in the subcontract. The parties to the subcontract would then be main *Supplier* as Purchaser (X) and Supplier (Y) as *Supplier* respectively.

It facilitates management of the subcontract if a person equivalent to the *Supply Manager* in the main contract is appointed in the subcontract.

To avoid confusion, in these notes, the terms set out in the table below are used.

SC main contract	*Purchaser*	*Supplier*		*Supply Manager*
SC as subcontract		*Purchaser*	*Supplier*	Subcontract *Supply Manager*
Terms used in this guidance note	*Purchaser*	Purchaser (X)	Supplier (Y)	Supply Manager (A)

The *Adjudicator* in the subcontract should be appointed in the same way as in the main contract.

Goods Information

The Purchaser (X) should prepare the Goods Information for the subcontract thoroughly to ensure that the subcontracted goods and services work is properly undertaken by the Supplier (Y) in accordance with the requirements of the main contract.

The following information about the main contract should be included in the subcontract.

- Title of the main contract Supply (Goods and Services).
- Name of the main contract *Purchaser*.
- Name of the main contract *Supply Manager*.

Supplier (Y's) programme

The Purchaser (X) should ensure that the information (dates, methods, timing, procedures, etc.) which he requires to be shown on the Supplier (Y's) programme is consistent with, and is such as to enable him to comply with, his own programme and other obligations in the main contract. These requirements should be included in the Subcontract Goods Information.

Payment

The payment mechanism is the Price Schedule which and this is the same for both the main contract and the subcontract therefore the arrangement is ''back-to-back'' and the amount paid to the Supplier (Y) is for the work in the Subcontract Price Schedule which the Supplier (Y) has carried out. Defined Cost includes payments for 'subcontracted work' and this is used for the assessment of compensation events (see below). If the main contract is ECC under Option C, the Price for Work Done to Date (PWDD) is in terms of the Defined Cost which the main contractor (Purchaser) has paid. Thus, before the main contractor can include payment for subcontracted work in his monthly invoice, he must already have paid the Supplier.

Compensation events

In order to allow adequate time for the involvement of Supplier (Y) in the assessment of a compensation event which affects the main contract, careful consideration should be given to adjustment of the time periods. The following additional conditions of contract, which are suggested as a guide, should be entered in the Contract Data for the subcontract.

In these conditions of contract the periods of time in the clauses stated are changed as follows:

- clause 61.3, second sentence, 'eight weeks' is changed to 'seven weeks'.
- clause 61.4, fifth bullet, 'one week' is changed to 'two weeks'.
- clause 61.4, last sentence, 'two weeks' is changed to 'three weeks'.
- clause 62.3, first sentence, 'three weeks' is changed to 'one week'.
- clause 62.3, second sentence, 'two weeks' is changed to 'four weeks'.
- clause 62.6, third sentence, 'two weeks' is changed to 'three weeks'.
- clause 64.4, fifth sentence, 'two weeks' is changed to 'three weeks'.

Disputes

A provision should be included to cater for a dispute arising under the main contract which concerns the subcontract. This enables the Purchaser (X) to require that such a dispute can be dealt with jointly with the dispute under the main contract by the main contract *Adjudicator*. This avoids two different adjudicators making different decisions on the same dispute.

The subcontract *Adjudicator* may be a person different from the main contract *Adjudicator*. His function is to deal with disputes which arise only between the Purchaser (X) and Supplier (Y) and which do not concern the *Purchaser*.

If any of the three parties to a joint dispute disagrees with the *Adjudicator*'s decision, he may refer it to the tribunal, as in the case of a dispute between only two contracting parties.

Insurance

By providing part of the *goods* and *services* as a subcontract, the *Supplier* in effect, passes to the Supplier (Y) those of the *Supplier*'s risks under the main contract which apply to work in the subcontract. Double insurance is largely avoided since the insurance premiums payable by the *Supplier* under the main contract will reflect the proportion of the *goods* and *services* which are subcontracted.

APPENDIX 5

Price Schedule

Entries in the first four columns in this Price Schedule are made either by the *Purchaser* or the tendering supplier.

If the *Supplier* is to be paid an amount for the item which is not adjusted if the quantity of work in the item changes, the tendering supplier enters the amount in the Price column only, the Unit, Quantity and Rate columns being left blank.

If the *Supplier* is to be paid an amount for the item which is the rate for the item multiplied by the quantity completed, the tendering supplier enters the rate which is then multiplied by the Quantity to produce the Price, which is also entered.

If the *Supplier* is to be paid an amount for an item proportional to the length of time for which *goods* and *services* are provided, a unit of time is stated in the Unit column and the length of time (as a quantity of the stated units of time) is stated in the Quantity column.

Item number	Description	Unit	Quantity	Rate	Price

The total of the Prices

                                    www.neccontract.com

APPENDIX 6

Contract Data – worked Example

Introduction

The following pages show the Contract Data completed for a fictitious contract. The purpose of this example is to help those unfamiliar with the NEC system to complete the tender documents. It should be read in conjunction with the notes included under the chapter 'Procedure for preparing a Supply Contract'.

The following points should be noted.

- The SC text of the Contract Data formats is reproduced as printed, together with the explanatory sentences which are in bold type. The explanatory sentences (e.g. 'Statements given in all contracts' and sentences beginning 'If…') are only for the guidance of users and should not be reproduced on an actual Contract Data.
- For clarity, quantities have been inserted in the appropriate places. **The figures given are imaginary and should not be taken as typical and certainly do not have the status of 'recommended by the NEC Panel'.** The examples of entries are not necessarily consistent throughout.
- Most optional statements have been completed so that users can see what should be written if that Option is chosen. **In a real enquiry only those statements relevant to the Options chosen should be completed.**
- If an optional statement is required it should be inserted in an appropriate position in the actual Contract Data, within the statements for the relevant section of the SC.
- **The statements in the boxes only provide a very abbreviated commentary on completing the Contract Data and should not be relied on.** Reference must be made to the conditions themselves and to the relevant guidance notes for a fuller treatment of topics.
- **The *Purchaser* must decide actual details based on the nature of the contract and the allocation of risk required.**
- **Those drawing up tender documents are advised to take care when completing the Contract Data that excessive risks are not passed to the *Supplier*. Common sense needs to be applied otherwise bids will reflect the unrealistic aspirations of the *Purchaser*.** In particular combinations including tight programmes, extended *defects dates*, large bonds, fixed prices, and heavy damages should only be used if the *Purchaser's* key strategy demands them.
- **The words of the SC Contract Data formats should be reproduced without change.** Users of the SC are granted a limited licence by the Institution of Civil Engineers to reproduce the text in tenders solely for the purpose of inviting, assessing and managing contracts.

Part one – Data provided by the *Purchaser*

Completion of the data in full, according to the Options chosen, is essential to create a complete contract.

Statements given in all contracts

1 General

- The *conditions of contract* are the core clauses and the clauses for Options X1, X2, X3, X7, X13, X14, X20 and Z of the NEC3 Supply Contract April 2013.

Choose any of the Options appropriate to the chosen contract strategy.

- The *goods* are

four heavy haulage tractor vehicles.

Describe the goods clearly but briefly. Full details of the goods will be included in the Goods Information.

- The *services* are

training and accrediting the *Purchaser*'s staff to drive and maintain the tractor vehicles.

As this title is likely to be repeated many times in correspondence it is sensible to keep it short.

The Purchaser's legal name and usual address are given here. The address need not be the registered office unless the applicable law requires it.

- The *Purchaser* is

Name   **Titanic Movers (Pty) Limited**

Address   **Plot H4678**

Gaborone

Republic of Botswana.

It is essential that the person chosen as Supply Manager is sufficiently close to the supply and has the time to carry out his duties effectively. He must also have sufficient authority to exercise the authority given to him under the contract.
See the guidance notes (GN's) on the Supply Manager.

- The *Supply Manager* is

Name   **Charles Atlas**

Address   **Private Bag X357**

Polokwane

Limpopo Province

Republic of South Africa.

- The *Adjudicator* is

Name   **Mr. I. M. Partial**

Address   **Court House**

Fair Lane

Cardiff

Wales, UK.

The Adjudicator proposed by the Purchaser can be named here, or a list of suggested names could be proposed here or in the instructions to tenderers. The most important aspect is that the Adjudicator must be acceptable to both parties. Care should be taken when choosing the Adjudicator – see notes on Dispute Resolution.

- The Goods Information is in

parts 2, 3 and 4 of the enquiry document.

- The Supply Requirements as part of the Goods Information, is in

part 5 of the enquiry document.

See GN on Supply Requirements which include an example.

- The *language of this contract* is **English**.

It is possible for the law of one country to be applied in the courts of another. Thus the place of jurisdiction should be stated here as well as the law that is to apply to the contract.

- The *law of the contract* is the law of **England and Wales** subject to the jurisdiction of the courts of the Republic of South Africa.

- The *period for reply* is **2** weeks.

The period for reply (see GN on clause 13) must be sufficient for the parties to respond, but should be sufficiently brief to maintain the principle of dealing with problems before they arise.

- The *Adjudicator nominating body* is

the Institution of Civil Engineers (London).

Care should be taken when choosing the Adjudicator – consider their relevant experience, qualifications and ability.

The Institution of Civil Engineers maintains a register of suitably qualified and experienced people to act as adjudicators. Several other institutions maintain similar registers.

The choice is usually between arbitration and litigation.	• The *tribunal* is **arbitration**.

• The following matters will be included in the Risk Register

The risk that parts of each tractor vehicle may need to be removed to allow it to pass through Border Posts.

The *Purchaser* lists here the risks that he requires to be included in the Risk Register. This alerts the tenderer to the risks, and encourages the *Supply Manager* and the *Supplier* to discuss how best to avoid or minimise their effects.

3 Time

• The *starting date* is **15 January 2014**.

• The *Supplier* submits revised programmes at intervals no longer than **5** weeks.

Making the period five weeks maximum allows for a 'normal' procedure, which is to have monthly revisions of a programme.

4 Testing and Defects

• The *defects date* is **52** weeks after Delivery.

• The *defect correction period* is **eight** weeks except that

  • The *defect correction period* for **an oil leak** is **one day**.

  • The *defect correction period* for **a breakdown which renders a tractor vehicle inoperable** is **two weeks**.

• The *defect access period* is **10** days except that

  • The *defect access period* for **class A Defects** is **Nil**.

  • The *defect access period* for **Defects in the Turbine nacelle** is **the period until the sea state is less than force 2 for greater than one day**.

This is the period within which the *Supplier* is liable to correct Defects.

There is little point in having an unreasonably short *defect correction period*. It makes for inefficient working on the part of the *Supplier*.

The *Purchaser* might require shorter periods for Defects that prevent his using the *goods* and/or allow longer periods for less critical Defects.

5 Payment

• The *currency of this contract* is the **United States Dollar (USD)**.

• The *assessment interval* is **5** weeks (not more than five).

The *Purchaser* should select a bank to reflect the *currency of this contract*

• The *interest rate* is **2**% per annum (not less than 2) above the **LIBOR rate applicable at the time quoted under the title "Money Rates" in The Wall Street Journal.**

The limit of five weeks is to ensure a reasonable cash flow for the *Supplier*. In practice most payment procedures will be based on calendar months.

8 Risks, liabilities, indemnities and insurance

• The minimum limit of indemnity for insurance in respect of loss of or damage to property (except the *goods*, plant and materials and equipment) and liability for bodily injury to or death of a person (not an employee of the *Supplier*) caused by activity in connection with this contract for any one event is **$5,000,000 USD**.

• The minimum limit of indemnity for insurance in respect of death of or bodily injury to employees of the *Supplier* arising out of and in the course of their employment in connection with this contract for any one event is **$5,000,000 USD**.

• The *Supplier*'s liability to the *Purchaser* for indirect or consequential loss including loss of profit, revenue and good will is limited to **nil (zero USD)**.

• For any one event, the *Supplier*'s liability to the *Purchaser* for loss of or damage to the *Purchaser*'s property is limited to **$500,000 USD**.

• The *Supplier*'s liability for Defects due to his design which are not notified before the last *defects date* is limited to **25% of the total of the Prices at the Contract Date.**

• The *Supplier*'s total liability to the *Purchaser* for all matters arising under or in connection with this contract, other than the excluded matters, is limited to **the total of the Prices at the Contract Date.**

• The *end of liability date* is **two** years after Delivery of the whole of the *goods* and *services*.

Unless the *Purchaser* has his own insurance department or access to insurance specialists, it is sensible to get advice on the figures to be inserted here.

This will be especially true when working outside the UK.

See GN on clause 88.

Optional statements

If the *tribunal* is arbitration

- The *arbitration procedure* is
  the Rules of Arbitration of the International Chamber of Commerce.

  See GN on clause 94.

- The place where arbitration is to be held is **Gaborone, Botswana.**

- The person or organisation who will choose an arbitrator
  - if the Parties cannot agree a choice or
  - if the *arbitration procedure* does not state who selects an arbitrator is

  the Chairman of the Joint Civils Division of the South African Institution for
  Civil Engineering.

If the *Purchaser* is to state the *delivery date* of the *goods* and *services*

See GN on clause 12.5 and clause 30.

- The *delivery date* of the *goods* and *services* is

goods and services	delivery date
Tractor vehicle one	**1 February 2014**
Driver training	**15 March 2014**
Tractor vehicle two	**30 June 2014**
Tractor vehicles three & four	**30 November 2014**
Maintenance training	**15 December 2014**

See GN on clause 31.1.

If no programme is identified in part two of the Contract Data

- The *Supplier* is to submit a first programme for acceptance within **four** weeks of the Contract Date.

If the *Supplier* is not to bring the *goods* to the Delivery Place more than one week before the Delivery Date

- The *Supplier* does not bring the *goods* to the Delivery Place more than one week before the Delivery Date.

See GN on clause 51.2

If the period in which payments are made is not three weeks

- The period within which payments are made is **six weeks.**

If there are additional *Purchaser*'s risks

- These are additional *Purchaser*'s risks

It may not be economical for the *Supplier* to assume a particular risk, especially a risk that has a low probability of occurrence but a very serious consequence.

1 **Delay in strengthening bridge 29 on the N27 Motorway.**
2 ....
3 ....

If the *Purchaser* is to provide any of the insurances stated in the Insurance Table

If the *Purchaser* has decided to provide any of the insurances, details should be entered here.

See GN on clause 87.1.

- The *Purchaser* provides these insurances from the Insurance Table
  1. Insurance against **loss of or damage to the *goods*, plant and materials**

     Cover / indemnity is **$6,000,000 USD**

     The deductibles are **$250,000 USD**

  2. Insurance against

     Cover / indemnity is

     The deductibles are

If additional insurances are to be provided

State any additional insurances to be provided by the *Purchaser*. This may include project wide policies and other special arrangements.

See GN on Section 8.

- The *Purchaser* provides these additional insurances
  1. Insurance against

     Cover / indemnity is

     The deductibles are

- The *Supplier* provides these additional insurances
  1. Insurance against

     Cover / indemnity is

     The deductibles are

If Option X1 is used

- The proportions used to calculate the Price Adjustment Factor are

proportion	linked to the index for	prepared by
0.40	Statutory labour table C-2	SEIFSA
0.10	Steel price table E-A	SEIFSA
0.40	Producer price (PPI)	Statistics South Africa
0		
0.10	non-adjustable	

1.00

See GN on Option X1.

- The *base date* for indices is **2 January 2014**.

If Option X2 is used

- A change in the law of **the Republic of Botswana** is a compensation event if it occurs after the Contract Date.

See GN on Option X2.

If Option X3 is used

- The *Purchaser* will pay for the items listed below in the currencies stated

items	other currency	total maximum payment in the currency
Tyres	Euro	€3,000,000

See GN on Option X3.

- The *exchange rates* are those published in

  the Financial Times on 2nd January 2010

If Option X7 is used

- Delay damages for Delivery are

Delivery of	amount per day
Tractor vehicle one	$10,000 USD
Tractor vehicle two to four	$5,000 USD per vehicle

See GN on Option X7.

If Option X12 is used

- The *Client* is

Name	Titanic Movers (Pty) Limited
Address	Plot H4678
	Gaborone
	Republic of Botswana.

See GN on Option X12.

- The *Client*'s objective is

  the delivery of capital plant to the Limpopo B project

- The Partnering Information is in

  Part 6 of the enquiry document.

If Option X13 is used

- The amount of the performance bond is **$4,000,000 USD**.

See GN on Option X13.

If Option X14 is used

- The amount of the advanced payment is **$1,000,000 USD**.

See GN on Option X14.

- The *Supplier* repays the instalments in assessments starting not less than **30** weeks after the Contract Date.

- The instalments are **10% of the payment otherwise due.**

- An advanced payment bond is not required.

If Option X17 is used

- The amounts for low performance damages are

amount	performance level
....	for ....
....	for ....

See GN on Option X17.

If Option X20 is used (but not if Option X12 is also used)

- The *incentive schedule* for Key Performance Indicators is in

  Attachment 1 to this Contract Data.

See GN on Option X20.

- A report of performance against each Key Performance Indicator is provided at intervals of **3** months.

If Option Y(UK)1 is used and the *Purchaser* is to pay any charges made and is paid any interest paid by the *project bank*

- The *Purchaser* is to pay any charges made and is paid any interest paid by the *project bank*.

If Option Y(UK)3 is used

term	person or organisation
....	....
....	....
....	....

If Option Y(UK)1 and Y(UK)3 are both used

term	person or organisation
The provisions of Option Y(UK)1	Named Suppliers
....	....

If Option Z is used

- The *additional conditions of contract* are

  in part 2 of the enquiry document.

The *additional conditions of contract* will become part of the contract, and so should be easily identified and logically located. Most people attach them to the Contract Data part one.

Part two – Data provided by the *Supplier*

Completion of the data in full, according to the Options chosen, is essential to create a complete contract.

Statements given in all contracts

- The *Supplier* is

Name	**SA Heavy Truck (Pty) Ltd**
Address	**PO Box 3017**
	Durban
	South Africa.

  Full legal name of Supplier

  Use the address from which the Supplier intends to manage the contract. This need not be the company's registered address unless the applicable law requires it.

- The following matters will be included in the Risk Register

  Availability of main gear steel forgings to meet manufacturing programme.

  See GN on clause 11.2(14)

- The *percentage for overheads and profit* added to the Defined Cost is **10%.**

- The *price schedule* is in **Document reference DSA/PS/01.**

- The tendered total of the Prices is

  $12,300,000 USD (Twelve Million, Three Hundred Thousand US Dollars).

  If the Purchaser has asked tenderers to insert this figure in the Form of Tender there may be no need to repeat it here, or alternatively read "The tendered total of the Prices in the Form of Tender".

Optional statements

The *Purchaser* should insert the appropriate optional statements for completion by tenderers before issuing the enquiry documents.

If the *Supplier* is to provide Goods Information for his design

- The Goods Information for the *Supplier*'s design is in

  Section 2 of the Tender Submission headed 'Design of Tractor Vehicle Drive Units'.

  If the Supplier is required to carry out design of all or part of the goods and to submit some details as part of his tender submission, his calculations and any drawings should be referenced here.

If the *Supplier* restricts access by the *Supply Manager* and Others to work being done for this contract.

- The restrictions to access for the *Supply Manager* and Others to work being done for this contract are

  Access to Areas 1 and 7 of the manufacturing facility in Durban is not allowed.

If a programme is to be identified in the Contract Data

- The programme identified in the Contract Data is

  programme reference DSA/Prog/T1.

If the *Supplier* is to state the *delivery date* of the goods and *services*

- The *delivery date* of the goods and *services* is

goods and *services*	delivery date

If Option Y(UK)1 is used

- The *project bank* is ....

- *named suppliers* are ....